Diary of a Secret Drug Addict

Addiction, dependence and recovery.
An ex-user's guide to breaking free.

Diary of a Secret Drug Addict

HARPER
element

The information provided in this book is for educational and informational purposes only and is not intended as a substitute for professional medical advice, diagnosis or treatment. Always seek the advice of your doctor or other qualified healthcare provider if you have any questions regarding addiction, or a medical condition or treatment you know you have or suspect you may have. All efforts have been made to assure the accuracy of the information contained in this book as of the date of publication. However, please note that medical information can change over time and you should always seek to verify current medical standards.

HarperElement
An imprint of HarperCollins*Publishers*
1 London Bridge Street
London SE1 9GF

www.harpercollins.co.uk

HarperCollins*Publishers*
Macken House, 39/40 Mayor Street Upper
Dublin 1, D01 C9W8, Ireland

First published by HarperElement 2026

1 3 5 7 9 10 8 6 4 2

© Secret Drug Addict 2026

Opening illustration by Dolly

Secret Drug Addict asserts the moral right
to be identified as the author of this work

A catalogue record of this book is
available from the British Library

ISBN 978-0-00-870984-6

Printed and bound in the UK using 100%
renewable electricity at CPI Group (UK) Ltd

All rights reserved. No part of this publication may be reproduced, stored in a retrieval system, or transmitted, in any form or by any means, electronic, mechanical, photocopying, recording or otherwise, without the prior written permission of the publishers.

Without limiting the exclusive rights of any author, contributor or the publisher of this publication, any unauthorised use of this publication to train generative artificial intelligence (AI) technologies is expressly prohibited. HarperCollins also exercise their rights under Article 4(3) of the Digital Single Market Directive 2019/790 and expressly reserve this publication from the text and data mining exception.

Contents

Prologue 1

1 They install the buttons 9
2 Brick in the wall 21
3 Come back to Camden 39
4 Out of control 61
5 Five years of drug abuse 73
6 Uncomfortable Christmas 83
7 I don't like the drugs (but the drugs like me) ... 97
8 Recovery – the first day 121
9 I seek professional help 151
10 Living with sobriety 165
11 Christmas Eve, New Year's Eve 197
12 The Secret Drug Addict 223
13 Manifesto 247

My Twelve Steps 265
Acknowledgements 271

Prologue

Prologue

THE BIT WHERE I AVOIDED WRITING THIS BOOK FOR AS LONG AS POSSIBLE

I've spent most of my life not writing a book.

This is important context.

If you'd asked me at any point before I reluctantly agreed to do this whether I saw myself as someone who would write a book, I'd have laughed my head off. I'd have deflected and asked you why on earth I'd do something so stupid. Writing a book was always something other people did. I know some people who've written books, and I'd never have grouped myself in with them.

I've never written one before. I feel this needs to be made really clear, early.

I've written tweets – now posts – on X. I've written a handful of articles on addiction and alcoholism for the press when asked (insistently). I've written captions, emails, text messages, notes to myself that say things like 'Don't forget' and are then immediately forgotten. But none of these things felt like training for a book. None of them involved sitting alone with my own thoughts, frozen solid with fear for extended periods of time. I'm now discovering that this is both the job description and the emotional obstacle course of writing a book.

And yet, here we are. You, holding this book. Me, having somehow survived the act of writing it.

The truth is, the process of starting this book was so nerve-wracking that I considered sacking it off several times. I wrote it collaboratively with my wife, who by some miracle didn't leave me to join a women's commune. She's also not a writer, so there were tons of arguments, door-slamming, times when she may or may not have called me several names relating to female genitalia – and this was her being reasonable and supportive. We live in a relatively small London flat and sadly didn't have a beach house or cottage in the Cotswolds where we could retreat to clear our heads and breathe.

A lot of this was written on buses, tubes, lunch breaks and late nights because we both work full time and have two kids and a dog at home.

Writing about your life is not like writing anything else. You can't hide behind research or fiction or structure. You are the subject. The content is your life. And, unfortunately, you remember too much and not enough at the same time.

★ ★ ★

PROLOGUE

From the off, my resistance was impressive. I resisted with commitment. I resisted with creativity. I resisted by convincing myself that I should first read every autobiography ever written, for research. I resisted by deciding I needed the *perfect* opening line before I could continue, as though the rest of the book would collapse without it. I resisted by re-reading my old tweets and thinking: *Maybe this is enough. Maybe the book is already out there.*

It's not.

What no one really tells you about is how vulnerable it feels to sit down and admit, in actual sentences, that you're a real person who has lived a real life, a flawed life, and is now attempting to explain it. Not justify it. Not polish it. Just explain it. To strangers. To people who'll read this in bed. On planes. In moments you'll never witness.

That realisation alone made me want to run away and call my publisher several times and say, 'Sorry, I can't do this.'

Because vulnerability is a strange thing. We talk about it as if it's aspirational, a lifestyle choice. As if it's a personality trait you can unlock with the right amount of courage and a well-timed deep breath. In reality, it feels more like standing in a room with the lights on too bright, holding a box labelled 'My fuck-ups', and slowly realising that you're the one who labelled the box and also agreed to open it.

Publicly.

★ ★ ★

I'm not unused to sharing things. I've shared *opinions* online. I've shared the fact I'm an addict, moments, jokes, observations, frustrations. But there's a difference between broadcasting fragments and assembling a whole. A tweet is a spark. A book is a sustained burn. A tweet disappears into a timeline. A book sits on a shelf and waits.

That waiting is terrifying.

There were days when I stared at my laptop and felt my brain would politely excuse itself. My thoughts scattered. Memories arrived out of order. Words hid. I'd think, *I remember everything*, and then immediately realise I couldn't remember what year something happened or why it mattered or how to explain it without sounding like I was a victim, bragging or apologising.

Trying to focus felt like herding cats – if the cats were memories, self-doubt and the sudden urge to google completely unrelated things. I'd sit down with the intention to write and suddenly feel an overwhelming need to look on eBay for an early 90s Spacemen 3 T-shirt or the Stone Island website for another coat, walk the dog, go to the gym, change the lighting, question my entire approach, check my phone 'just for a second'. That second would become twenty minutes. Sometimes an hour. Sometimes a very convincing argument that tomorrow would be better.

Tomorrow is always very confident. Ask my wife and publisher.

PROLOGUE

Writing this book required learning how to sit still with myself in a way I'd strategically avoided. It required trusting that if I kept going, something honest would eventually appear. It required resisting the urge to make everything sound smarter, smoother, more impressive than it was. It required admitting confusion. Admitting fear. Admitting that I don't always understand my own motivations until years later, and sometimes not even then.

There's also the small matter of memory. Memory is unreliable. Memory is selective. Memory has a fondness for drama and omission. Writing it means constantly asking yourself, *Is this how it happened or just how I remember it?* And then deciding that, for better or worse, how you remember it is the version you have.

That too is terrifying.

It also means choosing what to include and what to leave out, which feels suspiciously like editing yourself as a person. Some moments feel too small to matter. Others feel too big to touch. Some stories arrived fully formed, insisting on being told. Others hover at the periphery, unsure if they belong on the page or should remain safely unexamined.

I won't pretend I navigated this with grace. There were moments of confidence followed by long stretches of doubt. There were paragraphs I loved and then deleted. There were chapters I avoided writing until I absolutely had to. There were days when I felt strangely proud of myself for showing up, and others when I wondered who had let me do this in the first place.

If you're expecting this book to be the product of someone who has always wanted to write, I apologise. This is the work of someone who had to be dragged – gently, stubbornly – into the act of paying attention to their own life.

And yet.

Somewhere along the way, something changed.

The resistance didn't disappear, the fear didn't go away, but it became familiar. I began to understand that the discomfort wasn't a sign I shouldn't be writing this – it was the evidence that I was face to face with who I used to be. And I'm not that person anymore.

I procrastinated too long, missed the intimacy of it, but I had the feeling of pulling threads together and seeing patterns I hadn't noticed, the realisation that events I once thought were isolated moments were actually part of bigger pictures. The recognition that even the things I resisted remembering had shaped me in ways worth acknowledging.

I'm not presenting a perfectly coherent narrative of a perfectly coherent person. I'm certainly not that. This is an attempt to be honest about the mess, the contradictions, the learning-as-you-go quality of a life that didn't come with instructions or guidance.

★ ★ ★

PROLOGUE

If you find bits that feel uncertain, that's because they were. If you find bits that feel funny, it's because humour has always been my way of masking discomfort. If you find bits that feel exposed, that's because they were hard to write – and harder to keep.

I'm still a little uncomfortable knowing that you're reading this. That feeling hasn't gone away. But it's been joined by something else: a quiet acceptance that telling the truth – imperfectly, subjectively, humanly – is worth the risk.

So this is the beginning. Not the polished origin story. Not the highlight reel. Just the honest starting point of someone who didn't want to write a book, didn't think they could, and did it anyway.

If nothing else, I hope that counts for something.

Now, let's begin.

One

They install the buttons

My mind is out to kill me, and luckily for me, I know it. I am constantly filled with a lurking loneliness, a yearning, clinging to the notion that something outside of me will fix me.

My mind is my most dangerous enemy, my saboteur. It lies to me, tempts me into believing that annihilation is my only relief. It's out to kill me, and – strangely enough – I know it. That awareness is both a curse and my lifeline. The darkness isn't a shadow creeping, it's stitched into me, a lurking presence. I used to live with a nagging loneliness, a constant yearning, clutching at the fantasy that some external force – love, success, a substance, a distraction – would one day swoop in, pick me up and fix me. But of course, this was just my fantasy and nothing external ever did.

I've spent countless hours turning this question over: where does dysfunction really begin? Who planted the seed, the point at which unhappiness, chaos, addiction and the longing for oblivion take root?

When a person reaches for a bottle, a needle or a destructive relationship, what road lies behind them? And how far back can you trace that route before you stop seeing individual choices and start seeing inherited tragedy? In my family, it goes back generations. What I carry about is not just my own trauma but a twisted inheritance:

a strong, healthy lineage of mental illness, abandonment and bad choices.

In my own recollection, though, I can only really go back as far as my maternal and paternal grandparents. My maternal grandmother – she was always Pat. But later, in my thirties, I learned her real name was Helen. Names, like people, can be deceiving. She had a family once: a husband, two children, boy and a girl, and a house in Dundee, Scotland. From what little I know of her younger years she wasn't a particularly kind woman. Maybe she married too young, probably as a way to escape whatever home life she'd had before, and by all accounts she met her match in a man who was her equal in cruelty and indifference – he was a brutish, violent and arrogant alcoholic who was absent as much as he was present. There wasn't a maternal bone in her body, even that was apparent to me as a kid. So one day she decided she'd had enough. She packed her bags, left the house and never looked back. Escape is often the first move in families like mine.

Her children were left behind, abandoned, unfed and alone in that house until social services eventually came knocking. Children forgotten, as though they were toys a careless adult had grown tired of.

Imagine the wound that leaves: days of hunger and terror that etch themselves into your bones, then years of carrying the knowledge that your mother simply walked away.

THEY INSTALL THE BUTTONS

They grew up with those scars, eventually raised by their grandmother, but the damage was already embedded. The message they received was clear: you are unwanted, you are disposable. And that message, whether spoken or implied, tends to echo down the generations.

After abandoning her children, my grandmother reinvented herself in London. She got a job in a cabaret club called Murrays on Beak Street in Soho, by all accounts where she met my grandfather, Francis McGovern, and married again. This was the beginning of my mother's story.

My grandad Frank was from the East End. He was sharp-dressed and sharp-minded. He ran the Kaleidoscope Club in Soho, a place where the nightlife bled into something more shadowy. In the basement, Cantonese gamblers played mah-jong, the air heavy with the clicking of tiles and the muted exchange of cash. Upstairs, regular punters came for drinks. It was just a couple of doors down from the Krays' club, the El Morocco. He had dealings with them, but mainly with their brother Charlie. Frank knew how to get along with everyone without entangling himself too deeply. He wasn't a gangster, but he wasn't naive either.

Weirdly, Frank spoke Cantonese, which was unusual for an East Ender in the 1950s. The docks at Limehouse had brought a large Chinese community, and he must have picked it up as a kid. I read that he was responsible for giving the gambling community a start.

He was clever. He saved, invested, built a small property empire out of the club's earnings. By the time he died in the early 1970s, he left behind more than stories – he left a small fortune to my mum. That inheritance should have been a gift to her, a foundation to build her life on. But life doesn't always work that way.

On paper, my mum had everything: finishing school, ponies, the trappings of an upper-middle-class life. But none of that mattered. Adverse childhood experiences are not softened by material comforts. If anything, they sharpen the contrast. She had grown up with a mother who had abandoned children once and who could abandon them again. That kind of wound doesn't heal with ponies and pretty dresses. It festers. But inevitably, Pat and Frank's marriage ended, and for reasons unbeknownst to anyone Frank cut Pat off. It didn't take her long to move on to the next unsuspecting sod – Charlie, a lovely man who ran a fruit and veg stall on Kilburn market, was husband number three. He stuck around for a bit longer until she packed herself off to go and live on the Isle of Wight, leaving him on his own and needing palliative care.

We visited once, by which time she'd lost the plot, told my wife she moved there because when she'd go to visit the boys in prison she quite fancied living there.

THEY INSTALL THE BUTTONS

No idea who the boys were ...

My aunty told me a story about my dad. When he was first dating my mum, he would come around to the house. He knew she had money so was dogged in sniffing around her. He would call to pick her up and would delay making a decision about where to go on their date, by which time it would be too late and he would swerve having to spend any money on taking her out.

On marrying my mother, he saw himself as the natural heir to Frank's empire. He also fancied himself a property developer. How hard could it be, after all? Buy land, build flats, rake in the money. But arrogance and incompetence are a brutal mix. He didn't have a clue what he was doing, and slowly but inevitably the money trickled away. The land became a loss. The fortune dwindled to nothing. And even now, he carries no responsibility for it. He shrugs, deflects, rewrites history.

The land's in Stoke Newington and is now worth a fortune.

That failure poisoned my parents' marriage. My mother, who had never known safety or nurture, found herself shackled to a man whose dreams soured into anger. She hadn't learned how to choose well in love. How could she? Her own mother had abandoned her, then turned her away again when she came knocking for help. When my mother, pregnant with me, tried to leave my father, she tried to find refuge at her mother's house. The response she got was a door closed in her face and the cruel words: 'You've made your bed.'

Even when she attempted to take her own life, she was left on her own without her mother's support. That cycle of indifference, of cruelty, repeated again and again. I've still never had an honest answer from my father as to why she did this.

What chance did she have? She was repeating a pattern, copying what had been modelled for her. Monkey see, monkey do. Without ever having been nurtured, she had no idea how to nurture in return. She was desperate for love but gravitated only to people incapable of giving it.

My grandmother – Helen, or Pat, whichever name you prefer – was a toxic presence. She wasn't interested in her children, nor in her grandchildren. We were burdens, irritations, reminders of her own failures. And though I don't know much about her parents, I can guess the story. Hurt people hurt people. A woman who abandons her children is usually someone who was herself unloved, unseen. You can't pour from an empty cup, or so the saying goes.

My own survival was partly luck. I was offered therapy, almost a decade's worth, through the NHS. That gift kept me alive. Without it, I may not have become a husband or father at all. I may not even have lived long enough to tell this story. But many children are not as lucky. These cycles of neglect and dysfunction keep spinning, unchecked. Today's children inherit trauma like old furniture passed

THEY INSTALL THE BUTTONS

down in a will: battered, cracked, but impossible to refuse. And a succession of terrible governments has seen to it that the level of care out there now is so below average and inaccessible that this will roll on and on unnecessarily.

When I reflect on my father's role, I hear his words ringing in my ears. Once, I asked him why he never gave us guidance, why he didn't spend time with me or my brother. His answer was maddeningly dismissive: 'I knew you'd learn more from other people than from me.' He seemed genuinely confused by my question, as though fatherhood were a spectator sport. When I pressed further – 'Why did you have kids then?' – he shrugged. 'Because that's what people did.'

That shrug summed up my childhood. Children born out of habit, not desire. Parenting performed with indifference, as though we were chores rather than human beings.

I have my own children, but even owning a dog taught me more about responsibility than either of my parents ever did. Walking her, picking up after her – it's not always enjoyable, but it's what you do when you accept responsibility for a life. You show up with consistency and care, even when you don't feel like it. That's love in practice. Parenting should be no different.

My father was an only child, born in the aftermath of war, raised by a mother with schizophrenia. She was married to my grandad Joe, who was the most stable person in my life. He fought in the Second World War, in

Burma, and loved the horse racing. Steady and predictable in ways that mattered.

My father will tell you he had a terrible childhood. By all accounts, his parents adored him. Photographs show a boy who was loved, the centre of someone's world. He was mollycoddled by his parents throughout his life. If he hit a disaster, they would fix it for him; his car broke down, they'd buy him a new one. I'm not saying that this is what love is, but it's care and responsibility. None of which he inherited or learned to pass down. It got distorted along the way, didn't grow into the ability to give love. He inherited his own story, his own narrative, and it curdled into a bitter sense of entitlement.

Among the darkness, there were flickers of light. I remember one night vividly: walking hand in hand with my father down to Pang's, the chip shop in Kentish Town. We bought a bag of chips, steam rising, vinegar stinging the air. We went home, sat in front of the TV, watched *Spider-Man*. Chips. Cartoons. Dad. For once, happiness.

I thought it was a ritual, our Friday-night tradition. Later, my father insisted we only did it once. Maybe the truth lies somewhere in between. But that's how it is for children of absent parents; the rare happy memory grows until it fills the empty spaces, the way a single candle can light a cavern.

And then there are the other memories. I remember launching myself onto his back when I was four, full of

THEY INSTALL THE BUTTONS

excitement, expecting laughter. Instead, he screamed in agony. His back was bad. He shouted, cursed, doubled over in pain, and I froze. My joy had become a crime. I felt shame, confusion, the sting of being punished simply for being myself. That moment taught me something deep and dangerous: happiness is unsafe. Joy will hurt you.

Those are the buttons they install in you – buttons you spend a lifetime trying not to press.

Two

Brick in the wall

The best revenge is no revenge. Move on. Be happy. Find inner peace. Flourish.

I went to Primrose Hill School, which was in a quiet but vibrant part of London, just a stone's throw away from Regent's Park. It's a well-known area now, synonymous with actors and celebrities, but I suppose even back then it was a desirable place to live. It was well kept, its charming streets of Georgian terraces lined with trees, close to London Zoo. Over the years, the place has become more gentrified, and the school has, in a way, mirrored that change. Looking back, it probably had an air of being upper-class, even if it didn't feel like it at the time. The children I went to school with often came from homes that were tidy, well maintained and filled with the latest gadgets, but none of that really registered to me. It wasn't until I went to a classmate's house that I saw what privilege really looked like.

I remember going to the house on Camden Square, one of those grand three-storey houses, the kind with elaborate stucco facades and tall windows that overlooked a communal garden in the middle of the square, an oasis of calm and greenery in the middle of the city and a far cry from my own house. My friend's house was enormous in comparison, and stepping inside felt like entering a completely different world, each room more lavish than the last. It left me with a sense of unease about how others lived. I'd never seen anything quite like it.

At home, we lived in a much smaller, bustling house, crowded with stuff, kids and the usual noise that came with family. Our home wasn't special or pristine. It was lived in, functional and full of half-arsed jobs my dad never got around to finishing. It was a product of working parents. There was nothing in it that would make me feel uncomfortable or out of place, but visiting my friend's house made me realise there was a different kind of living altogether, something I'd not been aware of until then.

Growing up, I often felt like I didn't fit in with the other kids. I wasn't the typical boy, interested in the same things, talking about the same subjects. I was what some might call weird or awkward, different in a way that made it hard for me to connect. I remember having my own set of cutlery at school. I didn't want to share my knife and fork with the other kids, so every day at lunchtime I'd go to the headmistress's office to collect it like it was the most normal thing. She kept it locked away in her desk drawer. It was a small routine that set me apart from the others in a subtle, yet noticeable way, although the adults just saw it as an endearing quirk.

While the adults nurtured my foibles, the kids spotted them, sniffed me out. Kids have a way of doing this. It's like they've got an instinctive ability to target the ones that stand out. I was bullied from a young age physically and verbally. I was never in the right clothes, never had the cool things that everyone else had, but I was better than most of them at football, something they resented, and knew about things that mattered more to adults than to other kids. All of this made me an easy target, and my awkwardness only added fuel to the fire.

Every school day felt like a trial. It wasn't just the bullying that wore me down, it was the constant pressure to fit in, to act like everyone else, to be part of a group. Every interaction felt like a gauntlet thrown down, a test of my endurance. I couldn't put into words what I was experiencing, I didn't know how to explain it, and the adults around me were either too busy or didn't see it. The fear of retaliation made it harder to ask for help. My only response was to run, to physically escape whatever situation made me feel small or powerless.

Different things triggered it. Sometimes it was a fight in the playground, sometimes just the thought of having to stand up and speak in front of the class. My mind would race, my heart would pound, and before I knew it I'd be bolting down the street, running from it all, running from the pressure.

When I'd return home, my parents were rarely there as they were both working. I'd often sit outside on the doorstep for hours, waiting for one of them to come back. I was completely unable to deal with the constant mental strain; the social interactions, the expectations of school, the pressure to conform, everything felt like it was pushing me beyond my limits. I couldn't cope, so I withdrew from it all. I had no words for what I was feeling, but I knew I simply couldn't stay in that world for long. Fight or flight, they say. For me, it was always flight.

I was also a precocious kid, not only at school but in the general way I sought to control my little world. At the age of five or six when most kids I knew were being introduced to the culinary delights of Findus crispy pancakes and the now scrapped Turkey Twizzlers, I made a conscious decision to become a vegetarian. I still am, to this day. Maybe it was my way of wrestling some control over my life. My parents were strangely OK with this and didn't question it too much. Not many would have let their child make that kind of decision back then. They listened, and they let me be me; for that I'm grateful, but they should have pushed harder on the schooling front, though. All too often they allowed me to make important decisions on my own without much guidance.

In a world where I felt powerless, what went into my body was my choice, and it stuck. Through all the ups and downs, the addiction, the recovery, being vegetarian has been a constant. It's not much, but it's a decision I made and stuck to.

BRICK IN THE WALL

In school and at home I was a ball of anxiety. On the outside, I appeared quiet, maybe even shy. Teachers would have described me as reserved, the kind of child who did as they were told. But inside I was knotted up, a ball of tension I couldn't let relax. That tension followed me everywhere – into the classroom, the playground, and home at the end of the day. It sat with me during meals and at night when I tried to sleep. I didn't have the words for it back then; I only knew I felt restless, uneasy and different.

Nail-biting became my outlet. It was the one thing I could control, the one way I could release some of what I was holding in. At first it was just a nervous nibble, something small, barely noticeable. But over time it turned into a ritual. I'd bite my nails till they bled, a physical manifestation of all that was bothering me on the inside. I'd gnaw at them until there was nothing left, then start on the skin around them. It was like I was trying to eat myself alive, one fingertip at a time. It wasn't pleasant, but it gave me something physical to focus on, a sting I could measure against the vague, formless worry swirling inside me. It became a way of grounding myself, though I didn't think of it like that at the time. Looking back, it felt almost as though I were trying to chip away at myself one fingertip at a time, breaking the anxiety down into something I could see and touch.

The habit left its mark. Even now, when I look down at my hands, I can still see the evidence of those years. My nails never grew back the way they should have. There's a clear point where the growth stops, where the damage remains visible. It's become a permanent reminder of my childhood, one I carry with me everywhere. I don't notice it all the time, but every so often I catch sight of my hands and I'm brought straight back to how it felt to be that anxious child, trying to cope in the only way I knew how.

My anxiety didn't just stop at nail-biting. As I progressed through primary school, it grew heavier, shifting from a nervous habit into something far more consuming – panic attacks that could turn the most ordinary moments into trials I wasn't prepared for. These weren't the normal jitters people describe before a big event or the butterflies you get in your stomach before an exam. They arrived without warning, overwhelming and impossible to ignore. My chest would tighten, my heart would pound as if it were trying to escape, and each breath felt shallow, like no matter how much air I tried to take in, it was never enough. Alongside the physical sensations came an almost constant dread, a deep conviction that something terrible was about to happen, even when life was calm on the outside. In those moments, it was as though the walls of my world were closing in, leaving me with no room to move, no room to breathe.

These panic attacks didn't just unsettle me – they completely took over. One moment I'd be sitting in class, trying to concentrate on the lesson, and the next I'd be spiralling, my body reacting as though I were in real danger. My hands would shake, my breathing would quicken and my thoughts would scatter so quickly I couldn't hold on to any of them. The certainty that something was wrong pressed down on me, even when there was no explanation.

What made it even harder was not knowing what it was. I didn't have the language for 'panic attacks' at that age. All I knew was that my body was reacting in ways I couldn't control, and nothing I did seemed to help. I couldn't reason with it, I couldn't calm myself down and I didn't have the tools to fix it. That lack of understanding made it even scarier. I felt alone in it, unable to explain to others what was happening to me, unsure if they'd even believe me if I tried.

The unpredictability piled on another load of terrible dread. I never knew when an attack would hit me – whether it would be in the middle of a lesson, during a quiet moment at home or out in the playground surrounded by other children. That constant 'what if' became its own source of anxiety. Each day carried the possibility of collapse, and sometimes the fear of the next attack felt heavier than the attack itself. It was like walking through life with a shadow over my shoulder, never knowing when it would rear its ugly head.

Looking back, I see how much bloody space anxiety took up in my childhood. It wasn't just a passing worry or a stage I went through – it shaped the way I experienced the world. It influenced how I interacted with others, how I felt about myself and how I carried myself through each day. Even now, the traces are there. They show up without me even realising it, sometimes in situations where I know I'll be uneasy. I can prepare, but it takes work to act normal in those situations!

My already small world was closing in on me, the walls shrinking further in.

My mum knew that fundamentally something was not as it should be. She acted quickly and managed to get me therapy at the Tavistock, which was a big deal back then. Mental health wasn't something people talked about, so I'm forever grateful to her for having that insight and awareness.

The Tavistock Clinic in north London was a lifeline for many struggling children and families during the 1980s. Known for its pioneering work in child and adolescent mental health, it went on to help develop CAMHS (Children and Adolescent Mental Health Services). Unlike hospitals, it didn't just focus on treating symptoms – it went deeper into the emotional and psychological needs of the children who presented there. Heavily influenced by the likes of John Bowlby and Donald Winnicott, it was built on the foundation of psychoanalysis, exploring not just what children were going through, but why they were feeling and behaving the way they did. It also explored social factors, increasing awareness of the impact of poverty, racism and immigration on mental health.

It was one of the few places that recognised that emotional distress in children wasn't just bad behaviour to be disciplined out of them – it was something to be understood. For families who had nowhere else to turn, the Tavistock offered hope and a deeper understanding of how to navigate the complexities of their children's minds. It worked with kids who were self-harming or experiencing depression and anxiety, all of which were becoming increasingly recognised in the 1980s.

In my case, play therapy was used early on – I would draw pictures and play with toys rather than use words. They also worked with my entire family, which was quite pioneering at the time. As ever, my memory of time is muddled – I'm not sure how long I went for, but I do remember going there and drawing lots of pictures.

Those therapy sessions helped give me the tools to be a bit less impulsive and hot-headed. I remember the therapist telling me it was all right to stop and go back if I had one of my moments and ran out of school. Before that, I'd panic and think I'd fucked everything up beyond repair. It's funny how those words have stuck with me, all these years later.

That therapist, in her way, was trying to teach me that it's OK to make mistakes, that one fuck-up doesn't have to derail everything. It was a new concept for me, the idea that you could pause and turn around. Up until then, my world had been very black and white. Either I was coping, or I wasn't, and if I wasn't, well, game over.

Fast-forward thirty-five years and I gather they still offer the same advice to teenagers for when the world becomes a scary place. It's clearly a tried-and-tested exercise!

Try as I might I still found school challenging, so eventually my parents decided I'd be 'home schooled'. It lasted about a year, maybe a year and a half, and amounted to being given a dictionary to memorise by my dad. No proper curriculum, no structure – no maths, no science, no history. Just words. Random words that my dad thought might be useful. That whole period's a bit fuzzy now, like trying to look through a dirty window at my past.

At that time, something much worse was quietly taking root. I'd started to realise that if something was a bit shit – a situation, a feeling, a person – I could just opt out. No fuss, no confrontation, no tearful scenes. Just ... gone. Vanished. Like switching off a light. It started as something barely noticeable, but over time I became more conscious of this ability – and I refined it. Perfected it like a magician rehearsing a disappearing act. And when I eventually found myself neck-deep in addiction, it had become second nature, an art form.

Learning that you can just disappear – that you can disconnect, detach, shut everything out when the shit hits the fan – is a terrifyingly effective survival strategy when you're a kid. At the time, it feels genius. You're not causing trouble. You're not kicking off. You're just quietly removing yourself from the chaos. Floating above it all. It's a solution.

Except it's not. It's never really solved, is it? It just gets buried somewhere deeper. And while that escape route might have stopped me from having panic attacks or feeling like an alien on a planet I didn't ask to land on, it came at a cost. A quiet, creeping one. What I didn't know then was that these early coping mechanisms – the ones that felt like lifelines – were also laying down the wiring for every bad habit I'd carry into adulthood.

I got used to bolting. Emotionally, physically, spiritually – I was a master of the vanishing act. Relationships? If they got a bit intense or complicated, I'd check out. Jobs? One whiff of pressure or expectation and I was off. Friendships, responsibilities, even hobbies – if it stopped being easy, I was out the door before you could say 'commitment issues'. I'd just ghost life itself.

It took years – and I mean years – of sitting on therapists' couches, talking myself in circles, being dragged emotionally through the mud, to start unpicking that mindset. To see it clearly. To understand that avoidance might have once been necessary, but it had long since outlived its usefulness. It was doing more harm than good. At some point, you realise that every time you run, you leave another piece of yourself behind.

The real work – the hard work – has been in retraining myself to stay. To stay put when everything in me is screaming to leave. To sit with discomfort instead of fleeing from it. To have the awkward conversations. To feel the shit feelings. To not hide in a bottle, or behind a line, or inside some invented narrative where everything's someone else's fault.

And let me tell you – it's brutal. Because when your first instinct, your knee-jerk reaction to life getting messy, is to pull the ripcord and eject, staying feels like torture. You're fighting every fibre of your being. But that's the graft. That's the muscle you've got to build in recovery. Showing up when it's hard. Staying when it hurts. Choosing to be present, even when you feel like an exposed nerve.

In recovery, I've circled back to that lesson again and again – like a dog revisiting the same patch of ground, hoping it smells different this time. Trying not to think in absolutes, not to see every setback as a disaster. Trying not to catastrophise. Not to convince myself that one wrong move means it's game over.

You know what I've learned? However deep you've gone, however dark the spiral gets, there's always a chance to stop. You can't undo what's been done, no – there's no magic reset button. But you can limit the damage. You can stop it spreading. You can choose to turn the wheel, however slowly, in another direction.

BRICK IN THE WALL

It's taken me years to absorb that fully – to believe it with more than just my head. Because when you're deep in addiction, you think in extremes. 'Well, I've fucked it now, haven't I? Might as well carry on.' That thinking is poison. And yet it's seductive. It feels like logic. It feels true.

But it's not. Recovery has shown me that every moment is a fresh fork in the road. Every hour, every breath, is a chance to do something different. To change direction. It's not flashy. It's not instant. But it's real. You don't rewrite the past. But you get to have a say in how the story ends.

And if there's anything I've learned, it's this: don't let the perfect be the enemy of the good. That's what I used to do – hold out for perfection, then use its absence as an excuse to torch everything. But life's messy. People are flawed. And progress? Progress is ugly and slow and full of stumbles. But it's still progress.

I'm still learning that. Still fumbling my way through it. But at least now I'm staying in the room. At least now I'm not running.

In recovery, I've found myself circling back to the same idea repeatedly – like a moth to a flame or, more accurately, like a bloke stubbornly trying to force a square peg into a round hole, hoping that this time it might just fit. It's the idea that things aren't always as black and white as they seem. That a setback doesn't have to mean a full-scale collapse. That just because something's gone a bit sideways doesn't mean it's all gone to shit.

But here's the truth I've had to cling to like a lifebuoy: however far down the rabbit hole you've gone, however much wreckage you've left behind, you can still try to limit the damage. You can still turn things around. It's not glamorous. It's not some inspirational Instagram meme. But it's real. It's honest. And it's worth the effort.

It's never too late (there's the Instagram inspirational quote). Yes, it's a slogan that gets bandied about, but it's true. Life might not be perfect. In fact, it almost definitely won't be. It'll be messy and uncomfortable and full of things that don't go to plan. But that's not a reason to throw your hands up and walk away. That's a reason to get stuck in. You've got to work with what you've got – even if what you've got is half-broken and a bit wonky and held together with string and stubbornness.

You can't sit around waiting for life to get all shiny and pristine before you start showing up. That day never comes. And if you wait for it, you'll wait forever. And I repeat – don't let the perfect be the enemy of the good. It's annoying because it sounds too reasonable, but it bears repeating. Either way, it's the most solid bit of advice I've ever heard.

It's been a long road, learning how to live that way. Not just nod along in therapy or stick it in a journal, but to apply it – in real time, in the mess of real life. And it's hard. Because when you've spent years training your brain to think, 'I've fucked it, might as well double down,' it takes time to rewire that reflex. To pause instead of panic. To breathe instead of bolt. To say, 'Right, that was rough, but let's see if we can course-correct,' instead of immediately setting everything on fire.

In the depths of addiction, that kind of thinking felt impossible. It was all or nothing, sink or swim, and I always assumed I'd already sunk. I genuinely believed there was no point in trying to change anything because the damage had already been done. But recovery has taught me the opposite. It's shown me that every single moment – not just every day, but every hour, every minute – is a new opportunity to make a different choice. You don't have to wait for a clean slate. You just need to be willing to put your pen to the page again.

It doesn't erase what's come before. You can't go back and edit the past. But you can start writing a different ending. And some days, that thought is enough to keep me here. Still turning up. Still trying. Still choosing to stay.

Three

Come back to Camden

You have a little man, don't you? You have a little man who lives in your head and tells you when it's time to stop. Be thankful for that little man. Greater men have fallen through lack of one.

Francis Bacon

The Kentish Town I grew up in during the 1980s and early 90s really stood at a crossroads of old and new, tradition and reinvention, decay and creativity. Tucked between Camden Town's brash and (now) tacky energy and the refined affluence of Hampstead, Kentish Town possessed its own identity, forged by working-class resilience, a growing artistic undercurrent and the relentless churn of an evolving landscape that was becoming commonplace in London – and all over the country.

Kentish Town in the early 80s still bore the marks of its industrial and working-class past. Rows and rows of Victorian terraces, many of them carved up into rented flats, housed long-time Kentish Towners alongside an increasing influx of newcomers, ranging from Irish navvies to Afro-Caribbean families. Traditional corner shops and greasy spoons served builders in overalls, while market stalls along Queen's Crescent and the high street hawked everything from cheap clothing to fruit and veg, their vendors barking out prices over the constant drone of buses and the tube rumbling below ground.

Because of Kentish Town's proximity to Camden and central London, this made it a desirable, if slightly rougher location for those priced out of posher neighbourhoods. There were squatters in derelict buildings, turning them into makeshift homes and art spaces. Young professionals, encouraged by affordable housing, began to seep in, marking the slow creep of gentrification that would years later destroy the old community. But for much of my childhood, Kentish Town remained defiantly working class. Its pubs were filled with factory workers, bus drivers and the odd, ropey old poet nursing their pint of Guinness in the corner.

While Camden was fast becoming the epicentre of London's music scene – a place where I'd frequently hang out later – Kentish Town had its own gems. The Bull & Gate, a dimly lit Victorian pub with a sticky floor and a reputation for rowdy gigs, became a legendary venue for up-and-coming bands. I was taken to see the Housemartins there when I was a kid, bundled in under a coat. Later Blur and Manic Street Preachers would cut their teeth at the place, but in the 80s it was a haven for post-punk and alternative musicians looking for a space outside the more salubrious venues of central London.

Live music always thrived in these pubs. You could walk down the street on any given night and hear folk music coming out of the Assembly House and reggae booming from the speakers at the Tally Ho.

The rougher edges of the scene were found in makeshift venues, warehouses and abandoned railway arches where punk and squat gigs went on long into the night. They used to drive the neighbours mad, and I remember seeing the older lads come home from them. These types of nights had a really diverse mix of punks and students. The common denominator was that these were kids out for a good time, scraping by on the dole or student grants, united in poverty.

The influence of Jamaican culture was undeniable, with sound systems occasionally setting up on the street, and the deep basslines of reggae and dub pulsing through the neighbourhood. I lived across from the Kentish Town Afro-Caribbean youth club. There were thriving shops selling vinyl records imported from Jamaica, appealing to both local youth and DJs looking for the latest releases.

When I was a kid the streets were a blend of cultures, fashions and attitudes. Mods in sharp suits zipped past on scooters, their tailored suits in stark contrast to the punks with their studded leather jackets and gravity-defying mohawks. Some of the skinheads embraced the reggae-influenced suedehead look, but there were visible signs of the more aggressive right-wing extremists that plagued the era, often to be seen drinking in the pubs or standing about in clusters outside the betting shops.

There were fascinating-looking goths in flowing black outfits slumped around the tube station, chain-smoking and swapping cassettes of the Sisters of Mercy, while young lads in knock-off Adidas tracksuits and trainers loitered outside off-licences, flicking through the pages of *NME* or *Smash Hits*.

This was an area where the underground and alternative scene was thriving, fed by the energy spilling over from Camden and Soho, but Kentish Town retained a grittier, less polished feel, its subcultures less commercial, its rebellion rawer.

The streets themselves were always lively. You'd still hear the odd rag-and-bone men trundling their carts through the back alleys, calling out for scrap metal, and kids played football in the estates, their shouts echoing around the concrete. Now those estates have 'no ball game' signs up on them, so as not to upset the people who bought the flats in the right-to-buy era and sold them on to less community-minded and tolerant homeowners.

It always seemed to be a place that had political convictions. I remember seeing Socialist Workers Party posters plastered all over the place supporting the miners' strike up north or an anti-apartheid march down the high street.

Squatting and housing rights movements were strong in Kentish Town. There were many empty properties left to rot by absent landlords, and squatting became not just a means of survival but an act of defiance against the system that seemed to strangle the life out the working poor. Meanwhile, the rise in unemployment, fuelled by

Thatcher-era policies, meant that many young people were left to linger outside the job centre.

There was a strong Irish presence in the area; my wife had family that were long established in the area, like many others, but then there were the new ones, escaping the hardship of 80s Ireland or the Troubles in Northern Ireland. The Oxford Tavern was a pub where Irish folk music mingled with political discussions about the IRA, Maggie and the ongoing strife. Now it's an overpriced gastropub, and God knows what they talk about in there these days.

The police presence was often heavy, particularly after incidents like the 1983 Harrods bombing, which heightened tensions and led to increased stop-and-search operations in the area, targeting young Irish men.

Immigration did wonders for our introduction to 'world food'. We had kebab shops that sold us chips in pitta, and Pang's introduced me to curry sauce. You could get anything in markets like Queen's Crescent; they had cheaper produce, second-hand clothes and the occasional bootleg cassette. The older lot haggled over prices, while we spent our pocket money on sweets from corner shops that still sold them from glass jars lined up on the shelves.

As I got older in the late 80s, the first real signs of gentrification were beginning to become visible. Houses that once held multiple families were slowly being converted back into single dwellings, snapped up by professionals looking for a more affordable alternative to Hampstead. The pubs that echoed with folk music and rowdy debates in years gone by saw a quieter clientele moving in, writers, BBC employees and academics drawn to the area's proximity to central London and its anarchic bohemian charm. But for a time in my life, it was my neighbourhood and my community, and it still belonged to the people who had shaped it.

So it's no surprise that by the time I was twelve years old I'd discovered music, and it immediately became my lifeline. I fell in with an older crowd from school who were into the same music scene. My mates were sixteen and seventeen, worldly-wise in my young eyes. They started taking me to the Dublin Castle in Parkway, where bands like Madness and Blur played. A couple of record companies were based in Camden, so a lot of the bands hung out there. It was a cool little scene, buzzing with energy, optimism and possibility. Indie/alternative music in the early 90s was still quite underground, a secret language for the misfits and dreamers. If you saw someone with a copy of the *NME* or wearing a T-shirt of a band you liked, you'd gravitate towards each other like magnets. I felt like I was part of a secret club, a tribe of outcasts finding their own way.

On Saturday nights we went to the Dome in Tufnell Park, a mecca for music lovers and underage drinkers alike. One of my mates would be on the guest list, and I'd shuffle in to the middle of the crowd to get in. The place at the time was known for admitting underage kids, and anyway the 90s were more relaxed about that kind of thing. On a Sunday night, when the pubs shut at 10.30, we used to go to the Archway Tavern, a good spot if you wanted to carry on drinking to a soundtrack of shit chart bangers. You couldn't wear trainers, though. They were adamant about that! And in case you forgot, the burger guy outside would swap your battered Golas for a pair of oversized shoes so you could get in. If he wasn't there, or was out of shoes, you'd pull some black socks over your trainers and walk in looking like a fucking ninja.

Mid-week, we'd hit Syndrome at the bottom of Oxford Street. Andy, who ran it, managed Swervedriver, a band who were signed to Creation, pre-Oasis. It was a hub for young musicians and music journalists, a great little indie scene where everyone hung out, a petri dish of talent and ambition before Britpop exploded and changed everything. You'd be in the loo with a guy from Ride on one side and someone from Blur on the other, all of us pissing away our youth and loving every minute of it.

Being so young, I stood out like a sore thumb. A young thirteen-year-old in the pub watching bands ten years older than me, I was a curiosity. The music, the fashion, the attitude – it all became part of me, shaping who I was and who I'd become.

★ ★ ★

So that's how it came to be that I'd been out – and up – for three days straight: Thursday, Friday and Saturday night. By Sunday my head was pounding like a bass drum and my mouth felt like I'd been chewing on cotton balls. I called in at home, barely able to form coherent thoughts, let alone sentences.

'Is there any food?' I managed to croak out. 'Can someone run me a bath?'

I was knackered, my bones ached and my brain felt like it was trying to escape through my eyeballs. The phone went and my dad answered it. His voice was flat, emotionless. He put the receiver down, and as if he was about to tell me that we were out of milk, he said, 'Your mother's done a runner. She took your brother, and she's gone.'

My dad has a gift for delivery, I'll give him that. He'd have had the same bland tone and the same deadening lack of emotion whether the world was ending or he wanted a cup of tea. My mum had done a midnight flit, like her mother before her, and ended up in a women's refuge in Wales, leaving me behind with my dad.

The news hit me like a sledgehammer, but in my poor state I could barely process it. I just stood there, trying to make sense of the words that were still hanging in the air.

Understandably, he fell apart quickly after that. The house, which had never been a particularly warm or welcoming place, became a mausoleum to our broken family. I started spending even more time at my mates' houses, seeking my own refuge from the storm of my own life. Their home lives weren't perfect – whose is? – but they were more normal than mine, and that's what I craved. A sense of normality, a taste of what it might be like to live in a house where the walls didn't feel like they were closing in on you.

Three months passed in a haze of avoidance and escape. Then, one day, I was called in to the headmaster's office. My heart was pounding as I walked in, sure I was about to be expelled for something. But instead they handed me the phone. It was my mum.

I can't remember much of the conversation – again it's funny how memory works – but next thing I knew I was on a train to join her in Wales. And that's how, for eight months, I ended up living in Brecon. I mean, the Brecon Beacons were out back. You'd go out into the garden and there they were, looming up in front of you like some alien landscape. I never found out how she came to be placed in a small market town in mid-Wales. Maybe she wanted to get as far away as possible, or maybe that's just where the first spot came up and she took it. Either way, it felt like we'd landed on another planet.

The town was an odd mix. There were loads of squaddies mixed with ordinary town folk, weathered farmers and, more importantly for me, a cohort of bored teenagers. With that blend, the town centre was a fucking battleground, like one of those police action programmes. There were three pubs and a nightclub in a disused function room of the one hotel.

I was coming up to fourteen and caught between childhood and adulthood, belonging nowhere. The Welsh countryside, beautiful as it was, felt like a prison, and I couldn't settle. I missed London, missed the noise and the chaos and the familiar streets. Although I hated being at home with my dad, I missed hanging out with my mates and getting drunk, so I was back in the capital every weekend, going to gigs, chasing that familiar rush of noise and crowds and chaos.

The constant back-and-forth was exhausting, but it was the only way I could feel like myself. In Wales I was a stranger, an outsider. In London, even with all its problems, I felt like I belonged. The city was in my blood, its rhythms matching my own heartbeat. Someone once said to me, whatever you're into, however obscure or niche, you'll always find your tribe in London.

After eight months of life in the valleys, watching drunk Gurkhas fight and living in what seemed to be the inspiration for *Police Camera Action!*, trying to resist the pull of my life in London was like fighting gravity. I just couldn't fake it anymore – it was so obvious that, try as I might, I didn't fit in.

By the time I returned to London for good, my dad had completely lost the plot. The house was even more of a wreck and he was barely coping, just sitting in a patio chair in the front room, watching TV with the lights off. There was no furniture by then, and it's still a mystery as to where it went. He became unbearable. He drove family and friends away with his endless martyrdom, until he was basically radioactive. In therapy later on, I learned there's a name for this – projection – but it just made the world feel upside down. For my brother and me, the cruellest lesson was this: we weren't his priority.

My memories of my dad after my mum left aren't of his face, his voice or even his presence, but of the house that contained him. The house was basically his biography in smells: the sickly sweetness of food left to rot just long enough to be considered a science experiment, the damp that clung to your clothes – you know that smell, the one like you've left your stuff in the washing machine for a few days – and the dander of whichever unfortunate animal was crashing there at the time.

I knew this wasn't how normal people lived. Our house wasn't spotless when my mum was around – she wasn't running some Stepford kitchen – but at least it was *clean*. I'd visit mates and their homes would smell of dinners simmering on the stove, of furniture polish or that lovely crisp smell of freshly laundered clothes. Meanwhile, our house smelled like *neglect*.

When Mum left, the house collapsed in tandem with my dad. The dishes didn't just pile up – they fossilised. Bags of rubbish sat around inside for so long that the floor underneath turned tacky, like the kitchen had been converted into a fly trap. The washing machine broke, and instead of fixing it my dad invented a new system: leave damp clothes to ferment until they achieved a fine blue-cheese aroma. The bathroom grout turned black. The carpet grew crunchy, stiff with decades of spills that never fully dried.

The shame of it grew as I did. One day, a mate walked me to the door, sniffed the air and asked, 'What's that smell?' I shrugged, cheeks burning. After that, I stopped inviting anyone over. You can only pretend that eau de bin-juice is a new cologne for so long.

For my dad, the decay was never his problem. He had an easy scapegoat – 'Your mother abandoned us,' as if the mould itself was Mum's fault. The rot was literal and metaphorical, a perfect backdrop for his greatest performance – refusing to take responsibility for anything. Caring requires ownership, and ownership is something he never touched in his life.

If my dad had a gift, it was the art of blame. His work? He was a 'plumber', which mostly meant fixing the disasters from his last 'job' for a single landlord who owned a few properties. Each repair was a cover-up of the previous bodge job, like generations of bad DIY layered over each other. And again, nothing was ever his fault. His mum, his ex-wife, us, the neighbour's dog. The neighbours who actually *were* doing all right? Well, clearly, they'd only got there through crime or family money. Never mind hard work. That option didn't exist in his universe.

If he wasn't a plumber, he could have been teaching a masterclass in how to be the eternal victim.

The gas and electricity were always being cut off, and I remember shivering under blankets so thick I could barely move. One night, my mate Al left a glass of water on the side; by the following morning it had frozen solid. Indoors. The fog of my breath was a permanent feature in that house, like bad wallpaper. Showers? They involved going over to my mate Erol's, and his parents would 'just happen' to have enough food for me too. Only now, as a parent myself, do I see the quiet charity in that. Back then, I just knew their house didn't smell like despair.

When I asked my dad about the small matter of the lack of heat and hot water, he'd go off like a man possessed. He'd curse the utility companies, the government, the 'leeches' bleeding him dry. He never once admitted he hadn't paid the bills. No, it was all a conspiracy against *men like him*. Imagine being so special the gas board cuts you off just to make a point.

This went on for years, all through my early childhood, all through my teens. I was desperate for something resembling a normal family. Not perfect. Just … normal. I didn't know what 'normal' was, but I knew it wasn't dog-shit rolled in newspaper sitting in the hallway for three weeks.

One Christmas I cracked. I wanted the place clean, or at least passable. I had no clue what I was doing, but I went down to the paint shop on Camden Road, bought a 20-litre tub of white paint and some brushes, and tried to cover over decades of filth. You can't really paint over shame, but I gave it a go.

So I adapted. I also learned to cook cheap meals, wash my clothes in the bath, keep my mouth shut. Asking meant rejection, so I stopped asking. He lived in his grievances, and my brother and I became background characters.

Neglect doesn't leave bruises, but it cuts deep. The slow, relentless drip of 'You don't matter.' That was our inheritance.

And yes, he was depressed. But instead of fighting to get better, he used it as armour. Depression became another one of his excuses, his badge of victimhood. His illness wasn't something to heal from; it was his stage. Even years later, when my mum died, he brought her up in a row – still spitting venom about a woman who'd left him two decades earlier. My wife had to ask him to leave, and he's never been back since. Even then, it was everyone else's fault. Always.

Sometimes he'd lie in bed for days, drowning in his own despair – but the thing is, he wanted us to drown too.

We became more like flatmates than father and son, strangers sharing a space, circling each other without ever really connecting. I had free rein to do whatever I wanted, but the freedom felt more like abandonment. If I went out and came back at four in the morning, he wouldn't be waiting up worried and give me a lecture. If I didn't come back for two days straight, nobody cared.

It was terrifying and liberating all at once.

Now as an adult, I see it clearly. The narcissism, the depression, feeding each other like rats in a cage. His self-image too brittle to accept weakness, his despair recast as martyrdom. He wasn't just unwell – he was the universe's most tragic victim. Our needs didn't factor in. His pain filled every room until there was no space left for us.

As a child, I carried the invisible baggage of neglect every day. I learned silence was safer than need. That love was conditional. That affection always curdled into resentment. It made me fiercely independent, yes, but it left me hopeless with intimacy.

I don't feel anger so much as clarity now. He wasn't a monster. Monsters at least have presence. He was a void – consumed by bitterness until all that remained was blame. Depression was his shield, narcissism his fuel. Even now, I don't think he'll ever understand that everything ruined in his life was self-inflicted. His legacy is simple: blame. Mum for leaving, bosses for firing him, us for needing him. He's never taken responsibility for a thing.

My work has been to accept imperfection and to stop turning mistakes into martyrdom. His voice still echoes around me sometimes, whispering that failure means betrayal. But I answer with the truth he never grasped: failure is just being human. Growth takes ownership.

If he taught me anything, it was through absence. He showed me what happens when a man refuses to see beyond himself. He showed me the cost of self-pity. By blaming others, he modelled the corrosion of denial.

Dark as it is, that's his gift to me: a manual on how *not* to live.

I wanted to return to my old school, but at the time I didn't know how to make it happen. He wasn't helpful, and what kid knows a school admission process? So, for the second and final time in my life, I left school at fourteen. I got a job. I was a kid playing at being a grown-up, and there was nobody there to tell me what to do.

At fourteen, I started flyering for Syndrome – the club I'd sneak into. Flyering has to be the least glamorous job in the music industry, but you meet all sorts of people, and it's territorial, which was always entertaining. I watched some hilarious fights outside clubs when someone from Underworld dared to flyer outside the Camden Palace.

Imagine being a teenager handing out bits of paper to strangers who definitely don't want them, only to watch said strangers scrunch them up and bin them two feet away. That was me, a human recycling machine. But still, it was my first taste of being part of something that felt like *the industry*.

From there, Andy – bless him, a man who clearly saw potential in a scrawny kid who looked like he should have been in bed revising for GCSEs – gave me a job at Backstreet International, a music merch company. Lisa, his now ex-wife, was around too, and between the pair of them they gave me my first foot in the door. For me, this wasn't just casual labour, this was my in. I wasn't just folding T-shirts, I was *folding T-shirts in the music business*. I'd dreamed of working in music since I was twelve, reading music biographies like they were gospel. Kylie Minogue, Kraftwerk, Joy Division – my bibles. So even the faint smell of stale cotton mixed with cardboard boxes felt holy.

By some miracle – or clerical error – I landed a job talent-scouting for Sony when I was sixteen, having been interviewed by a man called Muff. I had no idea who he was, and it was only later I found out that he was a founding member, along with his brother Steve Winwood, of the Spencer Davis Group. To me he was just an adult in a suit.

I had no business being there. I couldn't even legally buy a pint, but I was being sent to gigs to spot up-and-coming talent. I had a bloody expense account! They'd probably have given me a car if I could drive.

I did a bit of everything: booked studios, ran errands, pretended I knew what 'A&R strategy' meant. In reality, nothing I did mattered – but I didn't care. I was in my element, absolutely buzzing to be anywhere near it.

It wasn't all glamour. Flying to Glasgow for a half-hour gig in a pub sounded cool in theory, but in reality it meant sitting alone in some five-star hotel eating crisps for dinner because I didn't know how to order food, and staring at the ceiling, wondering if this was really the rock 'n' roll dream I'd signed up for. And being young, restless and completely unequipped to handle the loneliness, the obvious solution was to drink and take drugs. Naturally.

By sixteen, I'd moved out of my dad's house and into a flat in Kilburn with a girlfriend. The road was actually called Shoot-Up Hill, which in hindsight was less of a quirky coincidence and more of a cosmic warning label. Moving out was supposed to be my great emancipation – no ghost of a dad skulking around the house like a character in a Dickens novel. And for a while, it was brilliant. The flat was decent, with a big shared garden. Back then, you could live in London without having a trust fund or selling a kidney. I was young, making money, had a girlfriend – it almost looked like happiness.

But good things and me never stayed mates for very long. Independence at that age sounds fun, but in reality it just meant I had more space to fuck things up in peace. There was no one to guide me, no wise mentor, no North Star. Even when I lived at home, Dad and I barely spoke; we were like two ghosts haunting the same house, each too awkward to acknowledge the other. And so, like every teenager with too much freedom and no real supervision, I made bad choices. A *lot* of them.

Growing up in the 80s, the big message was Nancy Reagan's slogan 'Just Say No', as if drugs were a piece of cake that you could politely decline at a birthday party. 'No thanks, I'll stick with the trifle.' For me, drugs filled in the gaps where love and stability should have been. They dulled the silence, gave me a false sense of belonging. It was like tossing pennies into a bottomless well: the sound was satisfying, but the well never filled.

Looking back, it's easy to spot the perfect storm: broken home, no guidance, too much freedom too young and the constant itch to crawl out of my own skin. Add in the music scene – that intoxicating mix of creativity, chaos and chemical temptation – and you've got yourself the recipe for a slow-motion car crash. It was salvation and damnation wrapped in the same package.

Addiction doesn't show up at the door looking like a villain. It doesn't announce itself with a cape and an evil laugh. No, it sidles up with a grin and says, 'Fancy an escape? A shortcut to belonging? A good time?' And before you know it, you're hooked, and what once felt like a friend becomes the parasite that strips you bare.

As I fell deeper into the world of music and drugs, I lost sight of who I was – or who I could have been. The little man in my head, the one Francis Bacon talked about, had long since been evicted. But somewhere deep down, hidden under all the wreckage, was a flicker of something else – a spark that wanted to survive.

That tiny spark would eventually save me, but back then it was buried under years of chaos, heartbreak and self-destruction. The road from there to any kind of salvation was long, ugly and filled with more pain than I thought one person could endure.

Looking back now, it feels like watching a film of someone else's life – one of those gritty indie movies where the protagonist makes *every* wrong decision and you're sitting there in the audience shouting, 'Don't go in there, you idiot!' But of course he does. Every time. That illusion of choice is a bastard. If only I'd done X, Y or Z. If only my entire childhood had been different. If only I'd had the handbook for how not to ruin your teens. But I didn't. I was winging it, armed with nothing but naivety, stubbornness and a hollow stomach full of warm lager.

So yeah, London called, and I answered. It nearly swallowed me whole, but it also gave me the tools to save myself. The music, the friendships, even the bad times – they all shaped me. And while I wouldn't wish that journey on anyone else, I can't regret it. Because without it, I wouldn't be here telling this story.

Maybe by sharing it, I can help someone else find their way back from the brink. Because if there's one thing I've learned, it's that no one is ever truly lost. So long as there's a beat left in their heart, I will never write anyone off.

Four
Out of control

The music business is a cruel and shallow money trench, a long, plastic hallway where thieves and pimps run free, and good men die like dogs. There's also a negative side.

After Sony I stumbled into Creation Records. I was eighteen and thought I'd made it. Creation! Oasis! Alan McGee! This was the stuff of *NME* front covers and student bedroom posters. One of my main gigs was still talent-scouting, which sort of sounds important but mostly meant me, terrified, standing in dingy venues half-cut, with other A&R scouts who had usually gotten their jobs because of their dads, uncles, family friends, worrying I was about to miss the 'next Oasis' or whatever, and ruin British music forever.

So I overcompensated. I was out every night, watched every band, drank every pint, took every pill and snorted whatever came my way. It was less 'A&R scout' and more 'young professional degenerate with an AAA laminate'. Within months I'd developed the kind of routine only an idiot could keep up with: all-nighters, straight into work, no shower, no shame. Picture it: me, at nine in the morning, plonked outside the office pavement, waiting for the manager to unlock the door. I'd have a warm can of Red Stripe in one hand, the metallic tang of last night's powder still dripping down the back of my throat, and all the glamour of a young adult who'd mistaken the 'music business' for the 'business of slowly killing yourself'. Honestly, I couldn't risk going home in case I passed out and missed work entirely. That was my idea of professional commitment – better to arrive stinking and twitching than not at all.

It didn't take long before the whole thing went sideways. By twenty-one, I'd unravelled. In a desperate, last-ditch attempt at cleaning up, I booked myself a DIY detox holiday. Greece, two weeks, on my own. Sun, sea, sobriety. Lovely, right? Except reality, as ever, has a habit of pissing on my chips.

I stepped off the plane and hit a wall of heat that felt like I'd walked into God's armpit. My plan was simple: no drugs. And, technically, I succeeded. But at that stage I thought alcohol was just a beverage. Not a drug. So my 'detox' consisted of trading adolescent cider-in-a-plastic-bottle for bottles of Bombay Sapphire. Sophistication! Progress! I'd drink myself into blackout most nights, staggering around the island like a one-man cautionary tale.

I even managed to crash a moped and hurt my back. Not exactly a holiday brochure activity, but honestly I've since met so many people who've crashed mopeds in Greece it might as well be a rite of passage. If you go to Corfu and don't stack a scooter into a wall, did you even really go? At the time, it felt like I was moving forward: fewer powders, more gin. Of course, I was still spiralling nose-first into the abyss, but now it was Mediterranean.

Back home, things came to a head. I got sacked from Creation. It was inevitable, really. My dream job, gone. One of the coolest labels in the country, representing one of the biggest bands since the Beatles, and I managed to balls it up. Shocking, I know.

I was twenty-one, and already washed up. That takes some doing. My shitty attitude – rolling in late, not working, refusing to follow instructions – didn't help. But truthfully, they'd been watching me implode for years. The cuts on my arms, the scabs and dried blood I never bothered to hide, the way I wore short sleeves like a walking cry for help. No one pulled me aside. No one asked if I was all right.

At the time, I felt invisible. Today, if my stepson showed up to work like that, I'd hope someone would intervene. But it was the 90s. Different world. Or, as my wife puts it, 'Ah, the 90s – there was no HR back then.'

When I wasn't working, I was hanging around flats, getting stoned like I had since I was thirteen. Half man, half boy, failing at both. I dipped in and out of independence like a nervous swimmer. Jobs, relationships, flats – I'd lose them all eventually, and crawl back to my dad's. It was absurd. A tragicomedy. Like Clov threatening to leave Hamm in *Endgame*, but more realistically Harold and

Albert from *Steptoe and Son* – stuck together, driving each other mad.

A lot of my mates were dealers, and hanging around with them was a non-stop party that, in our minds, would never end. We would steal cars, play our music super-loud and have kickabouts in the middle of the street – all while normal people were at work. We thought we were untouchable, invincible. In truth, we were just a bunch of twenty-something lads on the dole, living on scraps and hustles, like Del Boy if Del Boy had no ambition or charm. It wasn't sustainable – a house of cards waiting for the faintest breeze.

Every so often, I'd land another job and try to 'pull it together'. In music, you had to at least pretend to give a shit about the bands, which meant showing up to gigs. And I loved that part. Music was the only thing that made me feel alive, the one connection that cut through the fog. So I'd hit the shows, night after night.

Soon enough, I was out on tour, flogging merch, living the 'dream'. Except my version of the dream was nose-bleeds from too much coke, shagging anything that moved, and stumbling through days in a haze of groupies, powders and lager. It looked glamorous from the outside – the gigs, the travel, the buzz. But the reality? I was coming apart piece by piece.

I had the ability to bounce back quickly, though – or at least I told myself I did. That's the great lie of youth: you think you're made of rubber, able to ping back from anything, no matter how catastrophic. Youth is a hell of a drug. No hangover too bad, no disaster too final. You can burn through opportunities, health, relationships, and still convince yourself that there'll always be another shot waiting.

But, for some, there isn't. I watched friends lose their jobs in the industry during lockdown and struggle to get back in, over-paid middle-aged men who had failed upwards with little experience in an industry that made them feel like kings of the world. They were all unable to let go of their glory days, refusing to retrain and work elsewhere, still clinging to a life that was certainly on its way back. The reality was, however, that they'd been difficult to fire without massive pay-outs before Covid, and then Covid came along and gave employers an opportunity to get rid with a plausible reason, making way for younger kids who were easier to mould – and to pay less.

That's the thing about addicts, though. Some are chameleon like and seemingly manage. Some have the ability to work with what we have, to re-route the course of our lives, to change, grow and adapt.

That's where I'm lucky.

That summer, at Reading Festival – three days of mud, lager and questionable decisions – I ran into a guy from Mercury Records. We'd crossed paths before. He'd actually offered me a job once already, but back then I was too chaotic to seize it. This time, though, I was ready. Or at least I thought I was. Ready in the way only a twenty-year-old can be: overconfident, underqualified and still rattling from the mess I'd left behind at Creation.

He got me in without too much effort on his side, and just like that I had another foot in the door. I was shaken after what happened at Creation, but not shaken enough to actually learn anything. Reflection wasn't my strong suit in those days. I was still locked in to the same patterns, same excuses, same chaos – just accessorised with a slightly different laminate pass.

By the time I walked into Mercury, my drug use had escalated to the point where functioning was more of an optimistic concept than a reality. I could bluff it – that was my gift – but beneath the surface I was running on fumes, hangovers and the sort of bravado that only works when you're young enough to get away with looking like you don't care. My entire approach to work could be summed up as 'laissez-faire', a polite way of saying that I showed up, did as little as possible and coasted.

For about three years I drifted along at Mercury. I wasn't ambitious and I wasn't hustling. I didn't want to be the eager young exec desperate to climb the ranks. I was the opposite: the guy slumped at his desk, trying to focus through the fog, doing the bare minimum to avoid immediate sacking. If music was supposed to be my calling, I was treating it more like an irritating temp gig.

OUT OF CONTROL

Part of the problem was that the one person who had vouched for me – the guy who gave me the job – jumped ship to EMI pretty quickly. Without him, I was exposed. Nobody else in the office had much time for me, or my attitude. And why would they? I didn't go to the same universities as them, I didn't like what they were signing, I couldn't step out of my lane and – God forbid – actually sign a band.

I was rude, disengaged and arrogant in that special way you can only be when you've confused 'potential' with 'achievement'.

I also didn't have the faintest clue how to operate in an office environment. I'd never learned how to play politics, how to network, how to kiss the right arses without it looking like you were kissing them. Other people seemed to know instinctively how to navigate all that – the subtle alliances, the small talk, the unwritten rules. I'd missed that lesson at school. While everyone else was out in the playground learning how to negotiate and manipulate, I was at home, poring over dictionaries, memorising long, impressive-sounding words. Great vocabulary, terrible life skills.

The office itself didn't help. The fluorescent lights cut through my perpetual hangover like Stanley blades, amplifying the horror of every comedown and every sleepless night. The hum of photocopiers, the smell of cheap instant coffee, the endless parade of meetings – which could easily have just been memos, but everyone loved the sound of their own voices, everyone needed to keep their jobs, and that meant being visible and talking bollocks – the platitudes, the buzz words ... all of it made me feel like an alien trapped in a sitcom I didn't understand. I wanted the music industry I'd read about in biographies – late-night sessions, wild tours, electric gigs – not this sterile corporate version where you were judged on punctuality and whether your tie matched your shirt.

Eventually, there was a shake-up at the company – one of those restructurings where people you've barely spoken to vanish overnight and the atmosphere shifts like there's a storm rolling in. And I was out. Twenty-four, unemployed again, another bridge burned.

I didn't know it at the time, but that was the end of my music career. Just like that. No dramatic finale, no crash-and-burn headline. Just a quiet exit from an industry I'd spent my entire adolescence fantasising about. The dream had been right there in my hands, twice, and twice I'd let it slip.

If I'm honest, it wasn't just bad luck. It was me. My attitude, my arrogance, my inability to function, my refusal to take responsibility. Mercury was the final warning shot, the industry saying, 'We gave you chances, and you blew them. Off you go.'

At twenty-four, washed up and burned out, I should have just been getting started. Instead, I was already limping offstage, the house lights up, wondering what the fuck had happened.

It got ugly fast, and within a few years I'd completely unravelled.

Five

Five years of drug abuse

The next five years were dark. Not 'goth teenager writing poems in black eyeliner' dark, but the kind of dark where every morning felt like waking up inside a coffin you'd accidentally nailed shut yourself. I lost count of the number of times I came to in strange places, with no memory of how I got there or who the fuck was lying beside me. Sometimes it was a body. Sometimes it was just a smell – stale sweat, rotting takeaway, piss. Sometimes it was the scratchy carpet against my cheek. Always the same fog, always the same panic: *Where the fuck am I? Who the fuck is that? Who owns that dog?* and, most importantly, *Do I still have my wallet?*

That was the routine. The ritual. Start the night off with mates, everyone laughing, pints, pills and lines. Then, one by one, they'd peel off like sensible adults who had work in the morning. And me? I never had an 'off switch'. The night would stretch on endlessly, becoming a blur of faces and smoke and doorways. I'd end up in places I shouldn't have been with people I most definitely shouldn't have trusted. A merry-go-round of strangers, some friendly, some frightening, none of whom I clearly remembered in the morning.

The longer it went on, the more desperate and depressed I became. I tried to fill the void with anything that promised relief. Drugs, and alcohol obviously, but also antidepressants. I was about twenty when my GP first handed me a prescription, and I was clueless about the game of chemical Russian roulette I was about to start playing. That might sound ridiculous coming from someone who'd happily shovel anything into his body without knowing where it came from, but the thing with street drugs, you *know* you're gambling. It says it right there on the imaginary tin: this might make you feel incredible, but it also might kill you.

With doctors, it's different. You trust them. Especially at a young age, like how you're frightened of the police when you're a kid. White coat, clipboard, five years of university, serious face – you think they know best. But they're often parroting whatever the pharmaceutical reps have sold them. Foxes in the henhouse. My GP spent maybe three minutes with me. Asked a couple of perfunctory questions, nodded without looking up, handed me a prescription, and said, 'Here, try this.' And when you're drowning, you don't ask for the lifeguard's credentials. You just grab the rope.

Except this rope was wrapped around an anchor, and that anchor that was tied to a boulder. Within weeks of starting the pills, I was drowning in suicidal thoughts. Proper bleakness. Not just low mood, not just sadness, but a crushing, suffocating sense that life was unliveable. I felt like a puppet with its strings cut. Couldn't move. Couldn't think. The only thought I *could* latch onto was ending it, which terrified me as much as it seduced me. I'd battled depression before, enough to know it was serious. Enough to go looking for help, which, as a man, is already a cultural betrayal. We're not supposed to admit weakness, are we? 'Man up.' 'Get on with it.' Bollocks. But I wasn't ready for this.

I'd pace around my bedroom, Stanley knife in one hand, dragging the blade across my arm just to feel something. The sting of the cut was a relief compared with the numbness inside. Blood beading up, dripping onto the carpet. A porn video played on a loop in the background – the saddest soundtrack to the saddest ritual. I'd dial up girls, trying to talk them into coming over, then outright begging. Anything to interrupt the spiral. Anything to make me feel tethered, even for a minute.

The scars are still there. Thin white lines crossing my arms like a roadmap to nowhere. I catch sight of them sometimes, and it's like opening an old photo album – only instead of smiling faces and holidays, it's just reminders of the worst years of my life.

My girlfriend had long gone, had the good sense to get out in time, but living alone didn't help. There was no one to notice I wasn't myself. No one to point out how far I'd slipped. I never connected my crash to the pills – at the time, I thought it was just me, just my weakness, my failure. Then one night I caught a *Panorama* documentary about antidepressants. I nearly spat out my drink. 'That's my fucking drug!' I yelled at the TV.

It was like seeing your own house on fire on the evening news. This particular type was infamous for triggering suicidal thoughts, especially in young people. Doctors were dishing it out for everything: muscle pain, anxiety, depression, period cramps, probably bad hair days too. It was sold as a miracle cure, a pill for every problem. But buried underneath were risks: mania, dependence, weight gain and, oh yes, the small matter of wanting to kill yourself.

The pharmaceutical industry is a money-making machine, and when patients reported problems, they were often dismissed. 'It can't be the medication,' they'd say. Like telling someone lying in the middle of the road with tyre tracks across their chest that they must have imagined the car. I tried antidepressants a few more times in the late 90s and early 2000s, always clinging to the hope that this pill would be different. Each time, I stopped cold turkey. Not once did a GP say, 'Let's monitor you, let's taper this off.' It was sink or swim, and mostly I sank.

I later read a guide by a psychiatrist at the Maudsley Hospital who'd gone through the same hell, and he

FIVE YEARS OF DRUG ABUSE

explained how to come off these meds safely. Just as an FYI, cold turkey isn't recommended. But that's exactly what I did. When I finally ditched the pills, things slowly lifted. I was still an addict, still a mess, but at least I wasn't constantly thinking about killing myself. Progress, of a sort.

Since then, I've avoided antidepressants like the plague. I was lucky. Lucky not to get trapped in the cocktail-prescription spiral where one pill is given to offset the side effects of another, then rinse and repeat until you're rattling like a bag of Skittles. The cruel irony is that the drugs meant to save me nearly killed me. And, perversely, the chaos of addiction – always moving, always chasing the next high – might've kept me alive. When you're running full tilt, you don't have time to stop and let the monsters catch you.

These days, I look at the scars differently. They're not just reminders of pain. They're survival marks, proof that I fought battles and lived. My daughter once asked what they were, when she was really little. I told her they were from fighting a crocodile. One day she'll work it out.

I often think about the others. The ones who didn't make it. The ones still trapped in the numbness or, worse, who listened to the pills' whispers and ended their lives. That thought sobers me up faster than anything. Makes me grateful for every morning I open my eyes, even if it's not all sunshine and roses.

What saved me wasn't a pill, or even willpower. It was people. Connection. Finding others who could look me in the eye and say, 'I see you. I've been there.' Realising that what I was trying to fill couldn't be patched up with chemicals. It needed purpose. Meaning. Love. All the naff shit you roll your eyes at when you're young, but life and experience have since taught me that naff shit is really the only thing worth fighting for.

During those years, I'd get flashes of clarity, moments where I thought, *I can turn this around*. I'd get clean for a bit, find a job, straighten up. But it never lasted. The carousel always sped up again, and by the time I wanted off it was spinning too fast.

The anti-drug campaigns didn't help either. Leah Betts's face plastered everywhere, the 'Don't do drugs or you'll die' message hammered in. They thought it would scare us straight. It didn't. If anything, it made drugs seem more mysterious, more forbidden, more tempting. I'm not going to lie and say drugs can't be fun. Of course drugs can be fun. That's why people take them. Nobody ever says that out loud in campaigns, but it's true. A joint in the park with mates, a pill at a rave – it can feel like magic. So, when kids try it and have a good time, they start doubting all the warnings. 'What else are they lying about?' And from there, curiosity does the rest.

For most, it's a phase. For kids like me – damaged, restless, hungry for escape – it becomes a dangerous liaison. I

FIVE YEARS OF DRUG ABUSE

didn't have anyone to talk honestly with me about it. Didn't trust adults. Didn't have that kind of relationship with my parents. So, I made my own rules. The kind of rules that work until they don't, and by the time they don't, it's too late.

I liked the escape obviously, but I also liked the way drugs could make *anything* feel better. Nine a.m.? Get stoned before shopping. Tesco becomes an adventure. Doing my washing was great, those clothes spinning in the machine are pure theatre. Everything was either enhanced or numbed, whichever I needed most.

But the bad choices piled up, one after another, until I was buried under them. Each decision felt small at the time, insignificant. But they got messier and, together, they built a wall around me. And the higher it got, the lonelier I became.

Chaos can feel endless, but it's always heading towards a break. My break was coming. I could feel it, even then.

Six

Uncomfortable Christmas

Christmas in Britain in the 80s and 90s was impossible to escape. It was everywhere, dripping out of every shop window, radio station and TV set. From November onwards, the whole country lost their minds. Woolworths adverts promised mountains of toys and gadgets no family could realistically afford, all set to jingles that could rot your brain quicker than a bag of pick 'n' mix, and thick Argos catalogues doubled as wish lists – whole generations of kids circling pictures of Scalextric sets and Walkmans, convinced that Santa was basically a central supply manager at the retailer.

And the music – Christ, the music. Slade's 'Merry Xmas Everybody' blasting out of every pub jukebox, every cab radio, every cornershop till. Noddy Holder screaming 'It's Chrisssstmaaaas!' like a war cry, year after year. You couldn't move without bumping into Paul McCartney's 'Wonderful Christmastime' or Shakin' Stevens grinning like a man who'd just discovered cocaine and baubles in the same afternoon.

Then there was the telly. Every house in Britain tuned into the same stuff: *Only Fools and Horses* Christmas specials, *Morecambe and Wise* repeats, the Queen's speech if your drunk nan was in charge of the remote, Bond. Families would sit together, plates of turkey and Quality Street within reach, pretending to laugh at the same jokes. It was a ritual as predictable as the John Lewis advert is today.

Before my mum left, Christmas was a different experience. It wasn't perfect, it wasn't glossy like the catalogue version, but it had a warmth to it. The kind of warmth that lingers in a child's memory long after the wrapping paper's been binned. There'd be the smell of a nut roast that my mum had attempted to make for me because I was vegetarian, or sometimes a turkey crown filling the house, mixed in with the faint chemical tang of tinsel that had been dragged out of the loft every year since the 70s. The tree was always slightly lopsided, shedding needles like it had a terminal illness, but it didn't matter. To me, it was magic.

Mum made all the effort. She wrapped presents, even if they were just cheap toys or jumpers that didn't quite fit, she sang along to Christmas songs that came on the radio. There was chaos in the kitchen, steam fogging up the windows, the telly would be on in the background. It was messy, noisy, like the Christmases in my house now.

Then she left. And with her went Christmas.

UNCOMFORTABLE CHRISTMAS

Suddenly the house felt bigger and emptier like a church after everyone's gone home. No decorations went up, no Slade, no badly wrapped presents, no cardboard nut roast. It was shit. Christmas turned from something warm and messy into a hollow ritual. Just me and my dad.

Everywhere else, Christmas meant bustle, light and noise. At our house, it was silence. No bustle, no family traditions, just me and my dad, awkwardly sharing space.

The contrast was brutal. I'd sit there, flicking through channels, watching other people's scripted Christmas joy, and feel like I'd been dropped onto another planet. For everyone else, it was *togetherness*. For us, it was survival. Dad never quite got the memo. No crackers, no daft paper crowns, no games of charades. Just the sound the telly filling the silence. It was during those silent Christmases that the loneliness really took root. It wasn't just being without my mum or my brother. It was the realisation that the whole world seemed to be celebrating connection while I sat in an existentialist void. That contrast cut deep. It was like standing outside in the snow, nose pressed against a window, watching a party I'd never be invited to.

It made the loneliness sharper. Like sitting in a cold waiting room while everyone else was in a warm pub. And because Christmas was shoved in your face from every direction – adverts, music, TV, the whole cultural machine – you couldn't escape it. The country was one giant reminder that everyone else was supposedly happy, while you sat in your own private void.

Once I moved out, I never went home for Christmas again. My dad's house had by then descended into a tip and I couldn't stand the reminder of how shitty our lives were. I'd rather stay on my own, get off my face and pick up whatever food I could at the corner shop. It was as grim and as Dickensian as it could've been.

But while it was certainly bleak, I'd tell myself that I preferred it that way, that I was choosing to be alone. Deep down, however, I knew the truth. I was scared of feeling the crushing loneliness even when I was with people who were supposed to love me, so I'd hide away – just me with my drugs pretending the rest of the world didn't exist.

It always started the same. I'd wake up on Christmas morning, still half-cut from the night before, the room spinning, tongue glued to the roof of my mouth. That moment of panic would hit – *Shit. It's Christmas. Everything's closed. I've got nothing in.* The fridge would be empty except for maybe half a jar of pickled onions, a lump of moulding cheese and beer. Always beer.

So, I'd throw on yesterday's clothes, stumble out into the cold and shuffle down to the Co-op before the shutters came down. Those streets on Christmas morning always had a weird, eerie quality – silent, empty, like the aftermath of an air raid. Everyone else was indoors, warm, opening presents. I was out there, bleary-eyed, desperately

UNCOMFORTABLE CHRISTMAS

trying to cobble together a Christmas dinner from whatever dregs were left on the shelves.

The haul was always tragic. Pot Noodles, multipacks of crisps. If I was lucky, I'd find a mince pie or a bruised banana.

The staff knew exactly what was going on. You could see it in their faces when they rang through my pathetic excuse for a meal: pity mixed with disgust. Like, *Here's this sad bastard again, buying crisps and Pot Noodles*. I'd pay, mumble 'Cheers' and shuffle back to my house with my bag of misery, trying not to think about the fact that this was my Christmas dinner.

But the truth is, food was never the priority. Drugs were. I'd make sure I had my supply sorted weeks in advance just in case, God forbid, I had to face a sober Christmas. The Co-op scramble was an afterthought. My dealer at that time was my only Santa – minus the sleigh and reindeers, obviously.

The lengths I went to make sure I had enough to last over Christmas were ridiculous. I'd be planning it out in November, squirrelling away bits like some demented version of an elf. I wasn't worried about if I had cranberry sauce or a box of Paxo, I was worried about running out of gear. Starving was manageable. Sobriety was not.

And that's addiction in a nutshell. Everything gets inverted. Food, shelter, warmth, connection – all become optional. The only non-negotiable is the next hit. That becomes Christmas. That becomes life.

I'd sit there later, on my own, with a pile of crisps and biscuits on the table, tinny Christmas songs playing through the walls from neighbours' parties. And I'd tell myself this was fine. That I preferred it this way. But underneath, I knew the truth: it wasn't a choice. It was a cage I'd built for myself and then locked from the inside.

One year, a mate invited me over to his place in Muswell Hill for Christmas. A sweet gesture, really. He knew I was on my own, and he'd gathered a few other strays together – people without families to go to, the outliers, the ones who'd slipped through the cracks. It should have been comforting. But of course, I turned it into a full-blown ordeal.

The buses weren't running, which meant I had to walk. From Holloway to Muswell Hill – uphill the whole bloody way – in the freezing cold. Now, maps tell me it's a 38-minute stroll. But when you're high, paranoid and ducking into every other red phone box to snort a line, it becomes a two-hour epic. A trek through the Underworld, with me as the world's least dignified Odysseus, except instead of battling sea monsters I was wrestling with coke paranoia and trying not to lose my stash.

London on Christmas Day is eerie enough when you're sober. Streets dead. Shops shuttered. Even the pigeons seem to have the day off. But add cocaine into the mix and

UNCOMFORTABLE CHRISTMAS

it becomes surreal. Every shadow looked like it was moving, every distant sound sent me spinning around, convinced someone was following me. Streetlights flickered and hummed like they were conspiring against me.

And those phone boxes. Christ. They were like little confessionals scattered along the way. I'd duck inside, slam the door shut and rack up a line on the grubby ledge where once upon a time people actually put their coins. Each bump gave me thirty seconds of invincibility. Then I'd step back out into the cold, heart pounding, nose dripping, the loneliness hitting me again like a slap.

By the time I finally staggered to Muswell Hill Broadway, I was sweating through my clothes despite the frost, teeth grinding like I was chewing gravel, heart racing like a drum and bass track. I must have looked like a lunatic – gaunt, twitching, eyes darting everywhere. A walking advert for 'Just Say No'.

My mate had set up what was meant to be a makeshift family gathering. A few loners like me, some food, some drinks. On paper, it was exactly what I needed. A chance to not be alone. But I couldn't handle it. The coke had me on edge, and the deeper truth was uglier: I just didn't know how to belong anymore.

Even surrounded by other outsiders, I felt like an alien. They were laughing, chatting, clinking glasses, making the best of a bad situation. I sat there, rigid, watching it all through an invisible pane of glass. Every word, every glance, every laugh felt amplified, directed at me. The coke paranoia turned normal human interaction into something sinister.

It should have been a chance to connect, but it was torture. After a while, I couldn't stand it anymore. I made some excuse, probably mumbled something about needing a fag, and bailed. Slipped out into the night, back into the empty streets.

The walk home was worse. Darker, colder, lonelier. The coke comedown was kicking in, paranoia melting into despair. London was silent, but in my head it was deafening. Every step felt heavier; every shadow thicker. By the time I got back to Holloway I was broken.

That walk was a proper dark night of the soul. A journey that should have taken less than an hour became a kind of personal horror film – two hours of ghosts, shadows and the inescapable realisation that no matter where I went, no matter who I was with, I couldn't escape the loneliness.

Christmas was just the magnifying glass, really. It took everything I was already feeling – the loneliness, the dysfunction, the endless cycle – and turned the brightness up until it was blinding. But the truth is, those feelings weren't limited to Christmas – they bled into the rest of my life, every day of the year.

I'd look around at my mates, the ones who'd managed to dodge the traps I'd fallen into. They were moving on,

UNCOMFORTABLE CHRISTMAS

one milestone at a time: girlfriends meeting the parents, weddings, kids, mortgages, jobs that came with actual payslips and pensions. They were ticking off the boxes of adulthood, building lives, stacking bricks on bricks.

And me? I was treading water. Still chasing the next hit, still blowing whatever money I had on gear, still convincing myself that I had time. That I'd 'sort it out later'. But later never came.

The shame was overwhelming. Every time I saw one of them and they showed me a photo with their new baby or their first house, I felt like I was being left behind. Like everyone else had caught the train to the future, and I was still sitting on the platform, pockets empty, no ticket, no clue when the next one was coming. And the more ashamed I felt, the deeper I retreated into addiction. It became both shield and punishment.

Addiction's clever like that. It tells you it's your comfort, your escape, your mate who'll never leave. But really, it's the voice that says: *See? You're fucked. You'll never catch up. You're not like them. You might as well stay here with me.* It's seductive because it spares you the humiliation of trying and failing. If you never try, you never fail. You just keep circling the same drain, telling yourself it's safer this way.

The irony was, the lonelier I felt, the less I reached out. And the less I reached out, the lonelier I felt. It was a self-perpetuating loop, a snake eating its own tail. I became an expert at disappearing. Friends would invite me to places, but I'd decline, convinced I'd ruin it or be exposed for the mess I was. I didn't know how to be around people anymore. The coke paranoia, the booze, the self-loathing – it all built invisible walls around me.

So I watched from the sidelines while life happened for everyone else. It was like being stuck in the cheap seats of a theatre, watching a pantomime I wasn't part of. Except this wasn't funny, and I couldn't shout 'He's behind you!' because the villain was already inside me.

Every Christmas, that feeling doubled. The world seemed to pull away from me even faster, like a ship sailing off while I stood on the shore, too fucked up to swim after it. And the lonelier I got, the more I convinced myself I deserved it. Isolation became both the disease and the cure, until I couldn't tell the difference anymore.

Christmas morning has a way of amplifying whatever your life already is. If you're surrounded by family and laughter, it feels magical. If you're alone and adrift, it feels like the universe itself is mocking you. That day, it was a magnifying glass held up to my entire existence: the loneliness, the failure, the emptiness. Everything laid bare.

I cried for my mum, who wasn't there. I cried for my dad, who'd never really known how to be. I cried for the kid I'd been, the one who thought Christmas meant Subbuteo and laughter and warmth, not silence and pain. I cried for the man I'd become, half alive, stumbling from one fix to the next, convinced that was all I deserved.

UNCOMFORTABLE CHRISTMAS

I cried because I finally realised just how much I'd wasted. How much time, how much love, how much of myself I'd let slip through my fingers. For the first time in years, I couldn't hide from it. I couldn't drown it out with drink or coke. The truth filled the room, and I had no choice but to sit in it. That was the Christmas that broke me. I think of it now as one of the last acts before everything finally started to shift.

It was a turning point in the dark night of the soul. The moment when the darkness becomes so complete that, for the first time, you notice the smallest pinprick of light.

It would be another while before I got it, though.

Seven

I don't like the drugs (but the drugs like me)

My life in addiction always felt like I was being slowly strangled until I was turning purple and could barely breathe. It was so bloody insidious and slow-moving. I didn't have a clue how bad and out of control it was getting, since I didn't have the first clue about addiction and what addiction really was.

I thought I was just one of the very unlucky ones, the downtrodden, the underachiever – that this was just who I was, this was my life and I simply had to accept it. I certainly didn't know I could change it at any time. No one ever told me that before, and if they did I wasn't listening.

But here's another thing about addiction – it's a cunning bastard. It doesn't show its true face until it's too late, until you're in so deep you can't see the way out. It promises escape, belonging, excitement. What it delivers is isolation, shame and a hunger that can never be satisfied.

As I went deeper into this world of music and drugs, I lost sight of who I was, of who I could have been. The little man in my head – the one Bacon talked about – was long gone, if he was ever there to begin with. But maybe, just maybe, there was still a part of me that wanted to survive, that wanted more than this endless cycle of highs and lows. It was buried deep, yet it was there. And in the end, that small spark of hope would be the thing that saved me. The road to that salvation? It was long, dark and paved with more pain than I ever thought I could endure.

Writing this book has really made me look and think back to the first time I accessed drug and alcohol services to help me remember if I'd ever had recovery or abstinence suggested to me. It's a bit hazy as it was such a long time ago, but I seem to recall a pamphlet with details of Alcoholics Anonymous that I obviously never paid attention to.

The only conscious reference I knew to AA up to the point when I got to recovery was in the US police TV drama series *Cagney & Lacey*, although I couldn't remember which of the pair was the alcoholic. It wasn't the one who was married to Harvey, that I do know, so it must have been the blonde woman.

I have a black and white photo of the two of them in a frame by the telly. It drives my wife crazy, but I think it's hilarious. If anyone who doesn't know us comes to the house, I tell them it's my mum and her sister. The one with the dark hair is my Aunty Fran and the blonde one is my mum. I think the cultural reference is lost on anyone under forty, so I get away with it. It's a great photo, one I got from a shop I worked at in Soho for five minutes. My

I DON'T LIKE THE DRUGS (BUT THE DRUGS LIKE ME)

wife hides it in the cupboard regularly, although funnily enough she has never thrown it away. I think she must secretly like it.

I honestly didn't think I'd be using this example years later.

But that's the thing, I didn't know anyone in recovery – the word was alien to me in the context of drink and drug use. 'Recovery' to me meant recovering from an illness or a football injury. The words 'withdrawal', 'rattle', 'the bends', 'hungover', 'comedown' – these were words I associated with drink and drug use. My only knowledge of the word 'abstinence', just like 'celibacy', related to sex; its other meaning just wasn't in my vocabulary. I didn't have a clue!

So, Sharon Gless (yes, I did a bit of research) playing Christine Cagney was my first experience of an alcoholic in recovery.

Now you can't move for recovering alcoholics in the media. They're everywhere – writing books, making films, on social media telling us all how wonderful it is to be sober. It is, of course it is. I'm incredibly proud of myself, coming from where I did.

But I don't expect others to be as enthralled by my eighteen years out of the trenches. I left some carnage behind me that even I can't fix. I'm positive there are women out there who wish they could erase the bits of their lives in which I took up space.

Some leave out the nasty bits – the detoxes, the rehab stints, the manipulation, the selfishness, the stealing, the bed-wetting, the ulcerated legs through needle punctures, the lost teeth, the job loss, the abandoned families – but they do focus on the positives, like a Pot Noodle that you just add water to. Recovery from any addictive behaviour is not instant.

This is all great at promoting the cause. And it will appeal to a certain demographic, so if the message of recovery reaches someone this way, bloody marvellous.

Most of the people I encounter on X and Instagram have gone past the point where they can follow a plan to navigate Christmas office parties sober. They are the kind that don't get invited anywhere for Christmas, let alone have a job. They and their families are literally on the brink. You don't need that drink to fit in, but if you don't have that drink, you'll have a fit.

For me, the realisation that I was an addict didn't come like a bolt from the blue or a clap of thunder; there was no Carl Orff's *Carmina Burana* or some big, dramatic event associated with it. It was death by thousand paper cuts, it was the tiny inconveniences and dramas of my own creating that led me into a situation that had become like a vortex, and I was being dragged in by a very lazy disinterested version of the Kraken. It was just shit!

I DON'T LIKE THE DRUGS (BUT THE DRUGS LIKE ME)

No one had ever told me that I was an addict because most of my circle took as many drugs as I did, but, looking back, they had their shit together and they weren't addicts. This is rather common. Not everyone in your circle will tell you how bad you are, because chances are they are just as bad and telling you that you may have a problem might make them reflect on themselves, which is not always what they want to do. No one told me I was an addict because I didn't live on the streets or any of the other stereotypes that people have about addicts.

At first, like so many others, I thought I was enjoying it. Drugs had a way of making you feel that everything was going to be OK, and they made me feel like anyone other than myself. The drugs were an escape, a way to run from the carnage that was my so-called life.

I can remember those rare moments of bliss: a line of cocaine could deliver a rush so intense that I could feel something, a euphoric escape where I believed I was happy and fully alive, if only for a minute or two.

Over time the repercussions of my behaviour really started to mount up, ranging from the little ones to the big, huge, overwhelming ones. I couldn't kid myself any longer that I was OK. My life was an utter shambles. I was living a half-life existence that would now infuriate me because I try to fit as much as I can into my day, but at the time I felt like a bystander watching a slow-moving car crash. Every day of this half-lived existence was a blur of days merging into the next, a life of late mornings and a huge catalogue of missed opportunities.

I was always earning enough money to live week to week, but I was barely getting by, and certainly didn't have enough to enjoy any semblance of a decent life. I'd run a night here and there putting bands on, as I never let go of that – I still loved finding new music and wanted to share it with others; it was my way of connecting with like-minded people. I wanted to be in my life rather than watching from the periphery, but there were numerous barriers along the way and ultimately I'd run into problems with the people and those who ran venues, possibly because there was a sense of urgency and desperation about me. My motivation was different.

It wasn't that I didn't want to work; it was that getting out of bed was just too overwhelming. I would wake up past noon, endless days missed, and my body would be aching from the previous night's using. I was in my late twenties but my body was telling me a different story. I would see people that I'd come up the ranks with, whom I considered mediocre at best, go on to have successful careers, and would beat myself up thinking I was a complete failure. That bred bitterness and resentment, but not for one minute did I realise that I could possibly be the problem.

I wasn't a personality hire, I was an anarchist. I listened to bands that hadn't been invented yet and everything you

I DON'T LIKE THE DRUGS (BUT THE DRUGS LIKE ME)

like was shit, and I would tell you why it was shit. I didn't want to talk to you because you weren't interesting, and you had nothing to say to me that would make me change my mind. I didn't care who your dad was. But the tragic thing was, I was petrified, full of fear and I couldn't name it.

Just like school, work was a bit like banging a square peg into a round hole, and I never understood why until only recently.

Everyone around me was growing up, but I was stuck, because I had nothing and no one to grow up for.

The opportunities I was being given that could turn my life around became rarer and rarer, because I never treated them with any respect, and then the fear and overwhelm became suffocating. Like social housing and the people I took for granted, I thought they'd always be there.

My drug use was getting worse, my mental state was questionable. My appearance, well, I thought I looked all right, but looking back on pictures of myself from then I resemble a young Catweazle in a Prada jacket. The denial was that strong!

And all the while I still held on to the hope that everything would eventually fall into place, that the magic wand would appear.

★ ★ ★

My mum had been given the house by the housing association when she arrived back from Wales after years of being away. It was a five-bedroom house, and I'm sure that would never happen now – there are five people to a room in some families. She lived in it for a short period of time before realising that she missed Wales and went back there, leaving me in the house to take care of it with conditions.

The tension with my father remained palpable. When I needed help with my mum's house, which I was now renting, I was met with indifference. Despite his promise of helping with the upkeep on the agreement that the rent was paid on time, I'd call him in the hope he'd come over and help with the various problems the tenants complained about, only to be ignored with his style of passive–aggressive silence or ambiguous excuses. I read books, watched films and listened to music. I was in no way handy with anything that needed fixing: I didn't know one end of a radiator from the other, I couldn't set the boiler and had no idea where the fuse box or the stopcock was.

'Why can't he just fucking see that I'm drowning?' My frustration a symbiotic and bitter resolve to handle everything on my own. And I handled it badly.

As a parent, I wonder if my children showed such visible signs of struggle whether I'd stand to one side like a passive bystander. It's a difficult one to answer. I don't want them to grow up to be over-reliant adults, but I do want them to

I DON'T LIKE THE DRUGS (BUT THE DRUGS LIKE ME)

ask for help when they need it – and to not be frightened to ask for help.

Finding and paying the rent consumed me. Every Monday I had to have £170 to pay it at the Post Office. Due to my increasing drug use and unmanageability, my income was pretty sketchy. Heating the place was an absolute nightmare as the house was big, old and draughty, a five-bedroom property spaced over three floors. I drive past it a lot now because it's down the road from where I live.

I was trapped in a cycle of financial chaos. The housing association was relentless, and the constant fear of eviction was omnipresent, like a fucking rain cloud over my head. I'd spend night after night stressed, worrying about how to pay the bills while also trying to maintain a drug habit, never sure which one should really take precedence. I'd feel victorious when I could get it together, but this was always followed by the reality of having to go through it all over again the following week.

That house went from being a place of fun memories, filled with music, parties and people, a place full of hope and ideas – to a prison of which I was the chief architect.

During my addiction, I had shirked all the things that mattered: my relationships, they were mainly in tatters, or so I always thought; my responsibilities, these I was badly equipped to deal with; and, most importantly, myself –

well, I started to realise that drugs weren't really the fun escape they'd promised to be. They were a mask, one I even wore badly to avoid the reality of my situation. I started questioning everything. Was I really having fun, or was I just avoiding the truth? I don't need to think too hard about what the answer to that question was.

As the years went by, I wasn't that close to my mum, so I never thought Mother's Day would be the day when everything changed. But the universe has its own little ways of sending you signs. One day you leave the house, not knowing what lies ahead, and the next thing you know, it all changes and you have no idea how you got there.

I went out clubbing with a bunch of friends, nothing out of the ordinary, the usual drink, drugs, banging music and girls. Always girls. It was dark inside, the music was loud and bass-heavy, the type that makes you think your chest is going to implode.

When it was kicking-out time we stumbled out onto the street. There would be somewhere to go afterwards, someone who was up for carrying the night on always had a bedsit or flat – and if there were drugs involved, why end the night right now, so we invited some of the girls we'd met along to the flat where we'd decided the afters were going to be.

It was tiny, and there must have been at least twenty-five people all squashed into this cramped, sweaty hovel that reeked of fags and booze. Empty bottles and overflowing

I DON'T LIKE THE DRUGS (BUT THE DRUGS LIKE ME)

makeshift ashtrays were scattered all over the place, with people sitting on every available surface talking the shit that only gets talked when you're off your face.

Everyone was doing lines, having a laugh in the illusion that we were all connected, long-lost friends who had known each other since childhood, yet only meeting hours before.

The music was tinny, but loud enough that it drowned out any attempt at meaningful conversation, not that anyone was really that interested anyway. They were just waiting for the next high, lost in self-obsession.

It was chaotic, with everyone orbiting the coffee table, grimy, greasy, with a residue of white powder – the type of table you wouldn't put a cup of tea down on.

It was a good night, until it all changed.

This one girl, she stood out. I didn't know her, but she'd come back with the gang of people we recruited. There was something about her, with that mop of bleached blonde hair, an infectious laugh, a glint in her eye. I was intrigued. I watched her tap a line of coke onto the coffee table, lean down with ease, her blonde hair tumbling down around her face, and sharply inhale the line. She straightened herself up, tossed her head back, her pupils dilating so much that her eyes looked cartoonish. Then a trickle of blood seeped out from one of her nostrils, the red contrasting vividly against the snow white of her skin.

She started shaking and convulsing. I couldn't make sense of what was happening. I thought she was messing around, wasted. She fell from the chair, hitting the floor with a thud so loud it cut through the noise.

For a split second everything froze. The music continued but it was like it had been muted and the room was in slow motion.

Then chaos erupted, shouting, screaming.

I fumbled for my phone, trying to call an ambulance. My fingers stopped working, they didn't belong to me. I had been up for three days straight, my brain was frantic with exhaustion, adrenaline and cocaine.

I didn't know the postcode; I couldn't remember where in London we were. My hands were trembling so badly by this point that I could barely grip the phone, my mind went blank. I knew I was calling emergency services, but it was almost like I'd forgotten the number, the simplest of numbers. When I got through, I was in such trauma that I was giving them directions, but no full address. They weren't sending an ambulance without a full address, I was screaming for the address, which no one knew. Whose house was it? Blank stares. It was a live-action nightmare, and all the while this poor girl was convulsing on the floor.

Mixed with the panic of this, trying to get an ambulance and the feeling that I was totally out of my depth, was the need to get a hit to block it all out. This was the most real thing that had ever happened to me at this point of my life, and I was very badly equipped to handle it.

I DON'T LIKE THE DRUGS (BUT THE DRUGS LIKE ME)

My need to use, my desire to escape while a girl was dying at my feet is a shame that I carry to this day, my need to use overriding any sense of human decency or humanity. It was a stark consequence of my addiction.

Someone turned off the music so the sound of her vomiting and choking was amplified. People started to panic, rushing to grab their coats, some edging away muttering in shock. I shouted at someone to go outside to wait for the ambulance, an illusionary attempt at trying to take control of a situation I had no control over.

The ambulance arrived in what felt like hours, but really it was minutes. I looked on as the paramedics tried to save her, using defibrillators. It was like watching an episode of a hospital drama, but I was in the room. The noise still rings in my ears.

I took her friend into another room, still thinking I was in some sort of control. I said some comforting words, but really I hadn't a fucking clue what I was saying or doing. I was a mess, in no position to give unsolicited words of solace.

I was petrified.

I couldn't connect my brain and body; I was in shock and trauma and the reality that this girl might not make it was becoming more apparent, gauging from the noise the paramedics were making next door.

This was fucking insane.

How did it go from a fun night out to this? How the hell are we here listening to a bright, beautiful young woman being shocked in an attempt to keep her alive?

It wasn't all right. As we walked back into the room, they had lifted her onto a stretcher; she had passed. Her body lifeless and half-naked from the attempts to revive her. Her skin was grey and waxy, with the red marks of the defibrillator, and her eyes were half-open, such a contrast to the girl I'd seen less than an hour before.

Those of us who were left walked out into the street with her to the ambulance in the miserable grey dawn, but instead of going home to process what had just happened, to sit with the actual weight of it all, we rang some of the people who'd been at the party, the ones who'd scarpered and taken the drugs with them, and went around to their flat and just fucking carried on.

I remember the morning feeling crisp and cold, a shock to my system after the stuffy heat in the flat. The streets were eerily quiet. As the ambulance pulled away the siren cut through the stillness, a mournful wail that echoed the hollowness that I was starting to feel inside me.

It wasn't that we didn't care, it was that we didn't know how to care. We were trying to process what we had just witnessed as best we could with the paltry coping skills we had at the time. It was as if we were children playing at being grown-ups and we were completely out of our depth.

I DON'T LIKE THE DRUGS (BUT THE DRUGS LIKE ME)

As we started off in the direction of the next house the world and I started to wake up. Light and shadows cast felt like an image of the sun rising over the earth that you'd see in a science fiction film. Those moments are usually beautiful, but all it did was illuminate the reality, the awfully sad reality of what just happened, a reality I felt like I was trying to escape.

The world was too bright, too loud, too vivid. The walk felt endless. Every car horn, every slammed door, every noise felt like a personal assault. I was waking up and coming down, it was creeping in slowly, along with a fearful dread, and it felt like it was leaking outwards from my gut.

When, finally, we reached our mate's place, which was a dingy flat in a council block, the lift was out of order. The lifts were always out of order.

We climbed the six flights of stairs that stank of piss the entire way up. My mate answered the door, eyes like piss holes in the snow; he was bleary-eyed and reeked of booze and weed. His flat was a shambles: empty cans and bottles strewn all over, the ashtrays overflowed, the curtains drawn against the encroaching day. The TV was blaring in the background, canned laughter, smiling presenters in primary colours a jarring contrast to the heavy silence that hung over us.

We didn't talk about what happened. We made ambiguous, vague references, shared meaningful looks, but no one wanted to be the one to say it out loud. Instead, we did what we always did and started all over again. We got wasted.

The first line walloped me like a train, the nostril burn, postnasal drip, the rush of euphoria – it felt familiar. For a moment, just a tiny moment, I could forget. I could forget the girl on the floor, forget the sound of the defibrillator, forget the look in her friends' eyes.

But it didn't last. As the day went on, the flat felt like a pressure cooker of anxiety and neurosis. Every knock on the door, every siren in the distance felt like standing on a cliff edge. We kept the curtains drawn, every now and then peering through the gaps, convinced that at any moment the police would come bursting through the door.

The cycle of coming up and coming down repeated itself over and over. Each time I snorted a line the high got shorter, the crashing down got harder. My jaw was aching from grinding my teeth, my nose was raw and bleeding, my heart was racing and was skipping beats. At some point someone put music on. It was heavy and drowned out the sound of our collective laboured breathing, the sound of sniffing, the occasional retch as someone's stomach kicked back against the chemicals they'd consumed. I walked into the bathroom and stared at my reflection; the mirror was cracked. I barely recognised myself: my pupils were blown, my skin was pale and clammy. There was dried blood smeared under my nose.

I DON'T LIKE THE DRUGS (BUT THE DRUGS LIKE ME)

I splashed water on my face. As I stepped back into the living room, the contrast hit me like a punch in the face. Here we were, carrying on as if nothing had had happened, like it was a normal situation we were in, while somewhere in another part of London a family was getting the worst news of their lives, some mother's daughter was breaking down, some dad who worshipped the ground his daughter walked on numb with the fact that their little girl wouldn't be coming home, not ever again.

The guilt hit, then a tsunami of nausea that didn't feel like it had anything to do with the drugs I'd taken. I stumbled out onto the balcony. I couldn't breathe, I needed air. The sun was high up in the sky by this time and the day was in full swing all around us. I could hear children below playing in the courtyard; their shrill laughter and screaming sounded light and innocent.

My mind went to my mum. We weren't close by then, and we hadn't been since I was much younger. But in that moment, I needed her. I wanted nothing more than to hear her voice, to feel her arms envelope me and I needed her to tell me that everything was going to be OK.

Even if that was a lie. For the second time in a few hours I found myself fumbling for my phone, my fingers as clumsy and as uncooperative as they'd been when I'd called emergency services earlier that morning.

It took me three attempts to dial her number, each ring feeling like an eternity. When she finally answered, her voice distant and tinny. I fell silent, I couldn't speak. The words I was trying to speak stuck in my throat; I felt I was being choked by the guilt, the shame, and the desperate and childish need for comfort.

'Hello? she said again. There was a tone of confusion and worry. 'Is anyone there? Son, is that you?'

I opened my mouth, I tried to form words, but all that came out was a sob, and then another and another, until I was crying so hard I was struggling to breathe. I cried with all the grief I had ever carried in my body. 'Son, what's wrong?' Her voice was stern with concern now. 'What's happened? Are you OK? Where are you?'

I couldn't answer, I couldn't tell her where I was or what I'd done, what I'd witnessed. I couldn't bring myself to admit to my mum or to myself just how far I'd fallen.

'I'm calling your dad. He will come and get you,' she said. 'Please, love, just tell me where you are.'

But I couldn't. I ended the call, sank down onto the cold concrete of the balcony; still the kids played below, and I found more tears. I cried for the girl, for her family. My own lost innocence. I cried until I was empty and hollow, wrung out like a dishcloth.

When I finally picked myself up from the ground and went inside, I knew I had to make a drastic change. I couldn't continue to live how I was living, skipping from one drama to a crisis, teetering on the edges of disasters.

I DON'T LIKE THE DRUGS (BUT THE DRUGS LIKE ME)

That day, that awful Mother's Day, was the first time I actually looked at myself, really and truly looked at myself, and I did not like what I saw one little bit. I saw a selfish, cowardly little prick who cared more about using drugs than a girl dying in front of him. It was the first time I realised that if I didn't change my life I would end up the same way, another statistic, another life needlessly cut short.

A few months before, I had split up with yet another girlfriend. I found myself aimlessly wandering the streets and pubs in Camden looking for her. I needed her to fix something for me, some crisis I'd probably created and couldn't manage, avoiding dealing with my own shit, which I had become quite adept at. Or I needed her to validate me in some way or another.

I remember the feelings of utter desperation and loneliness. I was totally lost.

I never found her that day, my search was futile, and to be fair she was probably at university getting on with her life. If my daughter chooses a man like I was back then, I think I'll send her to get her head checked. Or Antarctica. Either one of those will be a plausible option.

Who did find me, however, was exactly who I needed to find me.

That very day I was making my way back to God knows where, or to see who knows, probably around to my oldest pal who lived and still lives in Kentish Town, one of the only ones who truly knew me, cared about me and, rather importantly, fed me.

My phone rang. It was one of the lads I grew up with who'd just driven past me. He asked me to meet him further up the street.

I got into his car, my hood up over my head in blazing sunshine.

He asked me something I hadn't been asked in quite a long time.

'How are you? Are you all right?'

Two simple questions, but in that moment it felt like I had never been asked anything so complex in my entire life.

I broke down. I was far from all right.

Without saying a word, he got out of his car and made a phone call. This was not out of character for him, he did that a lot.

When he got back in, he rolled a spliff, handed it to me and said. 'Right, that's it, you're coming with me.'

I've known this guy most of my life and had nowhere else to be. No one was waiting for me to come home, so I wiped my snotty nose and tears and just said OK.

He dropped me outside a church hall and I thought, *Fuck, is it that bad that I must seek redemption in Jesus?* I know nothing about God and religion, and what little I did know I was sceptical about.

Thankfully I did not have to go in and sing songs about

I DON'T LIKE THE DRUGS (BUT THE DRUGS LIKE ME)

professing my sins and how Jesus saved me – not my bag, but whatever gets you through. I'll leave that to the other religious evangelists associated with recovery. There were other people standing outside the church hall smoking cigarettes, and if you know a twelve-step fellowship meeting, you'll recognise this as the universal sign there's a meeting in that church hall.

I went in and sat down, still stoned from the spliff in the car, but there were trigger words coming from the mouths of the people who shared their stories, and they had my attention.

I stood up and got a keyring, disappointed that there was no bouquet of flowers or a sticker that said 'I did great', like you'd get at the doctors before all the NHS cuts.

I felt a shift in me; the tiniest spark had been ignited against all the sadness and chaos.

I had made my decision.

Eight

Recovery – the first day

My first Narcotics Anonymous meeting was on 12 June 2007. I don't remember many dates so precisely, but the day I inadvertently admitted I needed help stands out.

It was about three months after that young woman lost her life – a turning point for me that made it clear to me that I had no control over my life. I'd always known that my drug use was problematic and that I had an unhealthy relationship with substances, but for the six months leading up to me walking into that community centre it had gotten so much bigger than me. That night really jarred me to the realisation that I was well and truly done.

At almost thirty, my life felt like a complete mess.

I had nothing to show for the years that had passed, no achievements big or small that I could take pride in. Just a row of burned bridges, failed relationships and missed opportunities.

I wasn't a functioning drug addict by any stretch of the imagination, I was a walking disaster.

Some people can manage to hold it all together, keep their jobs, maintain their relationships, be good parents. This was not my experience.

My experience was that the chaos grew until I couldn't pretend anymore that drugs weren't a massive part of all of my problems, rather than the solution I imagined or hoped they'd be.

My girlfriends were always fed up with me, to put it mildly, but I never realised how nuts I drove them. I was emotionally checked out, a ghost within my own life.

I didn't know I was an addict, but I would find myself in relationships with women who were ill equipped to understand and deal with the carnage I was creating, or couldn't comprehend what was actually wrong with me. How could I expect anyone else to understand what was going on for me when even I didn't even have a clue what was going on for me?

Unbeknownst to me I was setting my relationships up for constant failure. I had a fantastic knack for self-sabotage and would make my problems theirs, overwhelming the relationship until all the fun was sucked out of it. I made everything about me and my needs, not considering that relationships are a two-way street. I had no experience of a healthy relationship to use as a template, and no sense of accountability.

Work, whatever little of it I managed to get, wasn't any better. My boss was always on my case, and looking back I can't blame him. I'd show up late, completely exhausted from sleep deprivation and looking like I'd been dragged

RECOVERY – THE FIRST DAY

backwards through a bush, still half-cut from the night before. I'd sneak off to the pub at lunch and stay there for hours, sometimes not even bothering to go back to work. I don't know anyone who goes to the pub at lunchtime anymore, unless it's for lunch and it really involves actual food!

My boss kept me on for as long as he could, but inevitably he let me go. And I still couldn't see I was the common denominator in all my misfortune.

The more I used, the worse everything became – so the more I used. And that only provided more fuel to my ever-increasing victim complex. My life felt hard, every area of it, work, relationships and housing. My solution to all my problems was to simply avoid them.

I was convinced my drug use was a direct response to the problems that everyone was causing me and I would stop once everything got better.

Maybe a new girlfriend, one who didn't nag, one who was fun and shared my non-committal attitude to free love and my debauched tendencies, and a new job with a boss who would appreciate my laissez-faire, antihero approach to employment. Anything or anyone else to fix the problem, anything except doing something that meant taking responsibility for my own shit, anything except taking a bloody good, hard look at myself.

But it was getting more and more difficult to shift the blame.

The more I used, the more drugs took the stage front and centre, while relationships, jobs and all the other pesky obligations that require real effort faded into the background.

One of the few differences between using drugs addictively compared with alcohol is that you can get blind drunk, throw up all over yourself, and yet the banter is great the next day. You can blend in for ages, as everyone does it – the pub, weddings, football matches, funerals, festivals. You might not even realise you're drinking too much; you might think you're just keeping up. But addictively smoking skunk or snorting coke is a lot harder to hide; the smell and the constant sniffing sort of give it away.

Your mates at the pub might be knocking back pints, getting drunk and having a laugh, but you're on another planet, far too wired to blend in.

A lot of my friends would take drugs like ecstasy, but it wasn't a thing I understood. You pop a pill and then what? Sometimes the first one wouldn't work, so you'd take eight more to get to where you thought you were supposed to be, and by that stage you were gurning your face off, hugging strangers and telling them you loved them. I suppose what I'm getting at here is that you can become quite complacent quite quickly if you don't understand what the outcomes are going to be. You've got no idea that what you're really doing is building up a tolerance and increasing your using is becoming normalised.

RECOVERY – THE FIRST DAY

My thing, really, was smoking weed and snorting coke. I liked the rituals involved: the rolling of a joint, the tapping of lines. With weed I was convinced I'd mastered a great skill, one that I could travel the world and demonstrate on a stage at world conventions if required. All my mates agreed that I rolled the best joints.

When I first came to recovery you'd generally see older faces when you walked into an Alcoholics Anonymous meeting. The landscape has changed dramatically since then, but at the time Narcotics Anonymous had a younger crowd, because we burned out faster.

The effects show up earlier from doing certain drugs. Take crack, for example. I only tried it a handful of times, but my wife used it every day for over ten years from the age of twenty-one to thirty-one. She was lucky. The physical consequences for her were minimal; she never used heroin or drank too much, which saved her from a far worse fate. In her opinion, at least.

She also used to brag that she had all her own teeth. Crack destroys your teeth, and she was pretty smug about that.

She's tiny, five foot two, and to have survived the volume of drugs she consumed is nothing short of miraculous, so it does make me laugh when she mentions it. She does know how lucky she is, though, as her odds weren't great by the time she reached recovery. But she has her gallows humour and a very can-do approach to life. She knows what she once had and what she's lost, but she looks forward and just deals with what lies ahead.

A few years ago, she broke one of her front teeth biting into a sandwich from a well-known chain. She was devastated. Oh, the irony!

But rather than spend money on paying for a ridiculously overpriced implant, she spent the money on a new kitchen and got a fake tooth, which she frightens the kids with when they eat too many sweets.

To be honest, I'd never even heard of Narcotics Anonymous and so can't drop an amusing *Cagney & Lacey* anecdote in here. I had no idea what to expect that day my mate dropped me off outside the community centre.

Part of me was desperately clinging to the idea that I could find a way to control my use and actually enjoy drugs again, like when I was younger. 'Total' and 'abstinence' were not words I was ready to embrace. I had no idea what they really meant. I just wanted to get stoned or high without it all going to shit!

But here I was, sat in a room full of faces reflecting my own struggles. Some looked tired, some looked happy and healthy, while some looked perplexed, also not knowing what they were doing there.

All of them shared stories that echoed my own. I felt moments of clarity, mixed with chaos and laughter, and times where it seemed I was drowning in despair. I had a feeling of fear that maybe this was really the end, coupled

RECOVERY – THE FIRST DAY

with the inevitable acceptance that I was going to have to leave my old life behind.

What struck me most was how they talked about a time long past when drugs were just a laugh, and how they slowly morphed into something sinister. I couldn't help but think of my moments of euphoria, the times when I felt invincible, which always ended with a crash. After every party comes the clean-up, but I was always too high to notice, help or want it to end.

The thought of giving it all up continued to gnaw at me. I just wanted the fun back, the fun without the wreckage. But how could I reclaim that without losing everything? I was already making excuses, trying to tell myself that it wasn't that bad, I wasn't that bad. I was painting a false narrative for myself; I was in absolute denial.

But something got my attention. There was a guy at the meeting who described how drugs had messed everything up for him – how he always ended up using more than he'd meant to, how when he stopped he could never stay stopped and when he did stop for brief periods his thoughts were consumed by using. He also talked about his unhealthy relationships with women, how he went from one toxic relationship to another, and then using again to get some relief from the turmoil. It was a vicious circle.

I'd never heard anyone link their drug use to their personal problems so directly, and it struck a chord.

My issues with drugs and women were so enmeshed in my head like a tangle of Christmas tree fairy lights, I couldn't tell where one ended and the other began. It was all one big fucked-up knot. Listening to him, I realised I wanted some semblance of a normal life, whatever that was.

NA meetings celebrate sober anniversaries – multiple years, one year, eighteen months, all the way down to 'Is anybody at their first meeting or wants to commit to a new way of life?'

People were getting up to collect these clean-time keyrings (they do chips called 'sobriety coins' in AA), and everyone was shouting and cheering. The energy in the room was infectious, like a wave of hope washing over the room.

I can't remember if I was pushed or was caught up in the moment, but I stood up and took my keyring. It felt surreal, like my body knew what to do before my brain did. There's a video somewhere online of a little dog who wandered into a parade accidentally – the crowd are cheering him and he looks chuffed with himself. That's just how I felt, no idea what I was doing, no idea that this inanimate bit of plastic was about to change my life. It was a symbol, a little bit of white plastic that would serve as a reminder that I had a choice, one I didn't even know I had a few hours earlier on that day.

As I sat back down, my heart raced with a mixture of anxiety and relief. I was embarking on something new, a

RECOVERY – THE FIRST DAY

path I'd never envisioned. The knot in my head didn't untangle overnight, but that keyring with the gold-embossed words saying 'Just for today' sparked a flicker of hope. That was something I hadn't felt in a long time.

Maybe, just maybe, I could start to disentangle the mess within me and find a way to reclaim my life, one clean and sober day at a time.

The next day I found myself in another meeting filled with faces that were to become increasingly familiar, another room filled with pain, laughter and unfiltered honesty. This time I listened more intently as people shared their stories. One guy was trembling as he spoke about how he'd lost everything – his job, his family – but amid it all he'd found the rooms of a twelve-step fellowship, which had given him a chance to start to rebuild his life one day at a time. This was all resonating with me, and it was beginning to cut through the delusion that I could use drugs successfully.

After that meeting, people approached me again, asking me about myself, telling me about other meetings nearby and local to where I lived. I went to the next meeting, and then another and then another. It started to become my new routine, my new normal. I had nowhere else to be: I was working sporadically, no girlfriend, no real distractions. I had nothing else better to do as all my mates were busy living their own lives, so I got on with the task of going to meetings.

But as I said earlier, I didn't ever really think that I was truly going to stop using drugs. I just wanted to be more successful at it, and maybe get my girlfriend back.

I still had the twisted notion that I could outsmart addiction, which is mad because it's like thinking you can outwit gravity.

Addiction is an illness. You don't fight an illness, you treat it. Some people will talk about battling addiction, but I prefer the word 'treat'. I fought against addiction for years; if I just do a bit of this, a bit of that, with the right mix of Valium, coke and weed, it'll hit the spot.

My life was a shambles in every way imaginable, but somehow I could manage to calculate the number of drugs I could take without it being destructive. That was my attempt at 'fighting'.

I am baffled at just how deluded I was.

It really clicked for me when someone explained it was just like a peanut allergy. 'If you're allergic to nuts, you can't just eat two nuts.'

This made a lot of sense.

I started looking at my history with drugs, and coming to realise how long I'd been in denial. I'd been trying to manage it on my own, under the illusion that I had control over it, but I obviously didn't. It had nothing to do with willpower and control. It was accepting that I had a problem, one that was beyond my capability to fix on my own.

RECOVERY – THE FIRST DAY

With each meeting I started to peel back layers of my past. I listened to others share their stories – some heart-breaking, some inspiring, some hilariously funny, although to anyone outside they'd just appear confusing. We have this amazing ability to turn misery into a stand-up comedy routine. I have sat in so many meetings imagining I'm in a sitcom! The amount of talent, creativity and intelligence in the rooms of twelve-step recovery meetings is unbelievable. These are people who'd been ostracised by society, told they were useless, people with the lowest self-esteem imaginable, who were brought back from the brink of death. Or worse …

Of course, there were setbacks and tears, and days when I felt like I wasn't making any progress. But each day drug-free was a success. Each meeting attended, each temptation resisted, each honest conversation – they all add up. I still occasionally go to meetings, listen to the stories from people in early recovery and see myself in them. I see the fear, the doubt, the hope. I tell my story too, because I know that if it can help just one person it's worth it.

I started jogging everywhere. I was crazy with energy, like a Tasmanian devil, and I was doing two meetings a day. I'd get up, have breakfast and jog to meetings all over London; I'd then go for coffee with other members, and before I knew it was off to another meeting in central London and a jog home afterwards. That's how I filled my days, doing way more than the ninety meetings in ninety days that the NA suggested.

It became easy – I liked the routine and it gave me a purpose. The realisation that we were all there for a common goal created a sense of camaraderie. This new mindset allowed me to embrace my vulnerability, which paradoxically made me stronger, sharing my feelings honestly rather than hiding behind this façade of ego and bravado I had created. The ego and bravado that had kept me sick for years.

The shift from isolation to connection transformed my outlook. I was no longer seeing myself of a victim of circumstance.

I totally immersed myself in the recovery community. I took on service positions within the meetings, which involved making the tea (badly), buying the biscuits and welcoming newer people. I began to understand that my journey wasn't just about abstaining from substances; it was about rediscovering who I was without them.

The hours I was initially struggling to stay clean turned to days, the days to weeks, the weeks to months.

Unbeknown to myself, I'd subconsciously surrendered to the fact that I couldn't take drugs anymore, I couldn't drink anymore and I couldn't behave badly anymore. I obviously physically could do so, but if I did I'd never be able to control it.

RECOVERY – THE FIRST DAY

I was a work in progress – and progress does not equal perfection. I had a lot of work to do around my behaviours with women. I wouldn't use myself as an example of how to behave around relationships in early recovery; I was more your poster child of what not to do.

I'd given up on the idea of picking and choosing the bits of recovery that I thought served me, and weirdly I didn't feel like I'd lost anything. There was no more thinking I'd just pick up a few hints and tips, then return to my life shiny and new. Recovery is all or nothing for me – it's headfirst, no half-arsed measures. There is no tweaking.

Recovery can act like an anchor for me. No matter how good or bad my week is, I know I have a place to go and listen, identify and count my blessings. It took me a long time to start forgiving myself, but I had a sponsor who helped me see that I suffered from an illness, and you can't blame someone for being sick. You just help them get better.

My life began to change in ways I didn't think possible. I started to mend some of the relationships I'd damaged. I never got back with that girlfriend, but I acknowledged and apologised for my behaviours and for the shit I'd put her through. She then promptly blocked me from every area of her life, and I've never seen her since.

But doing this stuff was a huge step towards becoming the person I wanted to be. Although there were a lot of one step forwards, two step back situations, I was becoming self-aware enough to know that if I behaved like a twat, I was the one responsible for being a twat.

I was starting to work out when I was making mistakes.

About ten weeks into my recovery in Narcotics Anonymous, I faced a brutal wake-up call. Just when I thought I was starting to get my life together, reality turned up unannounced.

It was a Saturday morning, and I had crammed into a car with a group of fellow NA members headed to a conference in Bournemouth. These are gatherings of addicts from all over the country, like a recovery network meet-up.

Meanwhile, while I was off enjoying this newfound sense of community, one of my old friends was on the brink of a complete breakdown.

A guy I'd been living with – someone I used to use drugs with – committed a horrific act, breaking into his foster parents' house at night, and attacking and killing his mother while she slept. His father managed to survive only by pretending to be dead. It was shocking, to say the least. You think you know someone, and then they turn around and do something utterly unfathomable. The news shattered the fragile sense of security I was desperately trying to build up.

I had a big house – too big for just me. Like everything else in my life, it felt overwhelming. I rented out rooms to people, and the house transformed into a chaotic microcosm of my life: too large, too messy and filled with people I barely knew.

Over the years, a revolving door of friends came and went. They'd stay for a while, then move on to relationships and new adventures, leaving me behind. My mates used to joke that I was like Rigsby from *Rising Damp*, always stuck in the same place while everyone else moved forward. It's funny how a joke can cut deeper than a punch; each departure felt like another failure, a painful reminder of my inability to progress.

As more friends settled down, the dynamic shifted to friends of friends, and then friends of friends of friends. Eventually, my house was filled with older guys I knew from the pub. These were men in their forties and fifties whose lives had unravelled, heavy drinkers and drug users desperately clinging to their youthful chaos. It was tragic.

One of them was Stuart, a Scottish guy who'd just split from his partner – she struggled with heroin, and he was an alcoholic with his own drug issues. Together, they were a volatile mix, like nitric acid and glycerol; you always knew something explosive was going to happen, you just didn't know when.

At that point in time I was increasingly desperate for drugs, and Stuart became a source for me. That's one of the most devastating aspects of addiction: it distorts your values. You lose the ability to discriminate, and before you know it you're surrounding yourself with anyone who can help you get to that next high. Morals, standards and self-respect all vanish when you're in the grip of addiction, leaving only a hollow version of yourself.

We'd be sitting in the living room, doing drugs, hanging out. It'd be, like, one in the morning. The lights are off, the telly's on, flickering in the background. Stuart would be telling me stories about his time in the French Foreign Legion and fighting in the Falklands. He'd talk about people he'd killed while in the army, his voice flat and emotionless. I'd sit there, nodding along, pretending to be interested, not having a clue if he was telling the truth or just lying. Nothing really ever went in. If you're using drugs on a daily basis, chances are you'll get to know some crazy people – it just becomes normal – so this was just another string of conversations that would go in one ear and out the other. I'd nod and make affirming noises, but really I'd just be waiting for him to pull out his stash. Here's a middle-aged man telling me about killing people, and all I cared about was getting high.

Anyway, one weekend in August, about ten weeks into my recovery, I walked out of a Narcotics Anonymous meeting and decided to head towards Camden to find my mates. They were always in the same pubs, so I knew where to find them. I didn't have any recovery friends yet, so I'd still go to the pub and preach the sobriety gospel to anyone who'd listen. Bit rich, that, coming from me. And

RECOVERY – THE FIRST DAY

for the record, I wouldn't advise this; you can't sit in a barber's chair and not expect to get a haircut.

I wasn't in a rush, and the weather was beautiful, so I decided to walk. The smoking ban had just kicked in, so the footpaths were crowded with people smoking, drinking and laughing. There were all these women around dressed up beautifully, ready for a night out. The contrast between the joy all around me and my loneliness was stark.

I set off walking through the West End towards Warren Street, while everyone else – laughing and a bit drunk – was heading into the city. My journey, alone, in the opposite direction, felt symbolic of my life. Always on the outside looking in, a voyeur heading the opposite direction. I never managed to find my mates, so I eventually turned around and headed home, feeling more alone than ever.

The next morning, one of my housemates that I'd been looking for called.

'Stuart's on the run,' he said, his voice tight with tension.

At first the words didn't make sense.

'What do you mean?' I asked, my mind struggling to process the information.

'He's killed his mum. Stabbed his dad and killed his mum. His dad's in intensive care. And he's on the run.'

I was shocked, but not entirely. Stuart had been unravelling for months, his behaviour becoming increasingly unhinged. The signs were there, but I'd ignored them, lost in my own addiction.

The following day was Sunday. There was a small piece in the papers about Stuart, tucked away in the crime section. It was even sadder, as the couple he'd attacked had fostered him at ten, hoping to provide a fresh start. By all accounts they seemed like good and caring people. It shows you how difficult it is to rewrite early trauma.

Anyway, a few days later Stuart handed himself in at a Cornish police station. Apparently, he walked up to the counter and said, 'Oh, um, apparently, I hear you're looking to speak to me about a matter.' He was trying to act casual, like he'd been on holiday, like he wasn't hiding from the horrific act he'd committed. The police saw through it, of course, and he got nineteen years in prison. Nineteen years. That's a long time to think about what you've done.

This young girl died on Mother's Day, and now, a few months later, a flatmate of mine had gone and killed his mother. I mean, dear God. The body count in my life was rising, and I felt queasy. I remember thinking, *I don't want to do this. This is not what I thought life was going to be. I don't want to be around this shit; these people doing these things to each other and having these kinds of experiences.*

I thought I was going to be David Geffen or Ian Wright, run my own record label or play upfront for Arsenal. I thought I was going to do something, be someone. How had I ended up here, surrounded by death and violence?

RECOVERY – THE FIRST DAY

All of these events brought home the reality that I couldn't rationalise my addiction anymore. I couldn't keep pretending that I could manage it and live a normal life while surrounded by madness and violence, fuelled by drugs.

I figured that if I'm not with people using drugs, I'm probably not going to see anybody overdose or die again. If I'm not hanging out with maniacs, then I'm probably not going to experience this kind of shit. I know people who've lived their whole lives and never seen anyone die, who've gone their whole lives and don't know anyone who's in prison for murder. And here I was, collecting tragedy like some people collect stamps.

I vaguely remember making a conscious decision then and there that I was going to commit to recovery fully, rather than trying to find a way to manage my drug use. I still wasn't sure exactly what recovery would entail or what it required of me, but my life was clearly a fucking mess and I didn't want it to be like that anymore.

The path ahead was unclear, but I knew I couldn't continue down the road I was on. I threw myself into recovery with the same intensity I'd once reserved for using drugs. NA wasn't just a place to get clean; it became my lifeline, my new routine. I'd been in and out of drug services since I was a teenager, but it was when I started really committing to recovery that everything changed.

I wasn't just trying to get sober; I was rebuilding my life from the ground up. Those meetings became my sanctuary, a safe space in a world that suddenly seemed confusing and overwhelming. I treated recovery like a job, showing up daily, listening and learning, and doing the work. I was so broken, so emotionally damaged, that I needed the structure and support. For years, my life had been chaos, and now, finally, there was a sense of order.

I met people who understood, who'd been where I once was. They helped me see that addiction is an illness, not a moral failing. I couldn't control it, but I could treat it. Their stories gave me hope, showed me that change was possible even for someone as fucked up as me.

Initially, it was brutal. I was leaving one life behind without any new life to step into. I was lonely and craved connection. As I said, I sometimes felt so lonely and lost and alone that I'd come out of an NA meeting and go straight to the pub to find my friends, trying to talk to women and preaching to people about why they were probably drinking too much. If you're lucky, you grow out of that behaviour. I cringe now, thinking about how annoying I must have been. But because I was starting to feel good, I wanted to share it with everybody. A bit like vegans. They love to preach about the benefits of veganism, right? I was the same with sobriety. Proper annoying. I'd corner some poor guy at the bar and launch into a lecture about the dangers of alcohol. Looking back, I'm amazed I didn't get decked. And if you're vegan, please don't deck me. I tried it, but I like ice cream and it was well before the amazing substitutes were developed.

My previous attempts to stop using were always badly executed. I'd go to the pub with the best intentions of just having a couple of drinks with my mates, and with those couple of drinks my inhibitions and best intentions went right out the window.

I wasn't fully aware that alcohol was the catalyst for a lot of my drug use. I never considered that even though I drank alcoholically at times, I would have been considered an alcoholic.

After a few pints, I start lying to myself.

My drunk brain would start saying I'll be all right, but my experience tells me every time I do drugs, it's not just a little bit.

It all goes horribly wrong. I don't know what I'm going to do. Am I going to make it home and sit there grinding my teeth, or will I go for it, switch my phone off and be gone for a few days?

When I was drinking, any promises I'd made to myself about doing drugs slipped away faster than agreeing to hoovering the stairs at 2.55 p.m. when there's a 3 o'clock Arsenal match on the telly. Every time I tried to have a weekend of not doing drugs, I'd go out with no drugs and no intention of buying drugs – I just wanted to go for a few pints and go home in time for *Match of the Day*. I'd want to be clear-headed if I had things to do the next day.

Two pints in, I'd bump into someone in the toilets who'd offer me a line, and I'm like, oh go on, just the one, and the next thing you know, it's three days later, and I'm in a stranger's flat on the other side of London wondering what am I doing and who the fuck are these people?

So it would seem that I did have a problem with alcohol after all.

Looking back, I threw myself deeply into recovery, almost to the point of disengaging from everything else. If I were advising someone now, I would possibly gently encourage them to get back into the real world a little sooner than I did. Get a little more of a balance. However, for me, at that time, I needed that total immersion. I probably needed to completely break away from my old life, from all the drugs, the madness and the violence.

I often wonder about Stuart, about the young girl who died on Mother's Day. Their stories are intertwined with mine. Their tragedies became my turning point.

Narcotics Anonymous wasn't my first rodeo with addiction services, but it was my first encounter with twelve-step recovery.

I'd been bounced around different services since 1998. Back then, you at least stood a chance of your GP referring you to a decent addiction clinic, a stark contrast to the present day, when you're lucky to get an appointment with a GP in real life.

RECOVERY – THE FIRST DAY

I drifted through these services, not ready to commit, not really understanding the enormity of my situation and its consequences that would present themselves further down the line.

But I'm truly grateful for that support that I had access to for all those years; it prepared me for the later part of my journey.

One of the standout rehabs was City Roads, because that's where it was, by Angel in Islington. Everyone I knew went there. It's sadly gone now, a victim of spending cuts. You could call up, and if they had space they'd pick you up. This could have been within an hour or a couple of days at most. There was no messing about, no queues. It was a twenty-one-day detox, part of a comprehensive programme they provided.

After this was completed, they'd send you to rehab in a charming seaside town where you'd have a bit more time and freedom, and finally you'd be given a room in a supported sober-living house with other addicts for six to nine months, where you'd have daily group therapy and learn to be a person again.

There has been such a decimation of social and drug services that it's near impossible to get the help I was freely given. My GP was able to signpost me to excellent therapy and addiction clinics, but if you can't even get a GP appointment, and they can't signpost you to drug services because they run on fumes, what can they do?

They can't fix poverty, they can't prescribe a house with more rooms or sort out the dampness and the broken boiler.

It's like sticking a plaster on a broken leg. The services that have survived have less skilled staff; they're well meaning, but there won't be a doctor in sight. They might turn up once a week to prescribe methadone, Subutex, citalopram or some horrible antipsychotic to a long list of people. And the waiting lists are insane!

The turnaround is quicker than it should be and there's often no encouragement to reduce the substitutes they prescribe. They just manage the drug use; they push people out because the backlog is unmanageable and they cut all the costs. The effects that these cuts have had on people I've been in contact with over the years is nothing short of inhumane. It's just horrible.

For me, the former Conservative politician Sajid Javid, whom I will return to again later, summed up the attitude of the government, the one that inflicted the cuts to addiction services. He suggested that family members, rather than the state, should be responsible for helping people out of drug addiction because of the 'unsustainable finances' of the NHS – as if its financial state wasn't the fault of his own incompetent government. He said that his father stopped smoking simply because his mother told him, 'If you die, your sons won't have a dad.'

Javid proclaimed that 'whether it's stopping drug addiction or dealing with depression, there's no more powerful

RECOVERY – THE FIRST DAY

motivating force than family'. Sajid clearly never met mine, and what about the people who don't have any family?

This was one of the most irresponsible things I think I'd heard from that government. It's almost like saying to someone who has cancer, don't have that chemo, your dad is going to pray for you. Who in their right mind would suggest not having a lifesaving treatment?

Sadly, Sajid Javid's brother died by suicide in 2018.

I received a lot of help from the Margaret Centre, a service based in north London. It was outstanding, in my opinion, a complete lifeline. The staff were incredibly compassionate, you felt like they cared and had the time to give you. A bit like the people I met in Narcotics Anonymous years later, they wanted me to do well – I could feel it. That made a huge difference: the feeling that someone cared about you when you barely cared yourself whether you lived or died.

The Margaret Centre closed in 2023, another casualty of a government with a hard-on for austerity. They offered me rehab in my twenties, but when they explained that rehab meant total abstinence, I wasn't all that enthusiastic. At the time, the idea of total abstinence seemed insane. The issue for me was a few specific drugs, cocaine mainly. The fact that I was smoking weed all day in my opinion wasn't a problem, in my mind at least. It was better than the alternative. I was happy sitting around smoking, so I stayed in the house. At that point I wasn't staying up for days on end, staring at the TV, destroying myself with self-inflicted malnutrition and insomnia.

By staying in the house eating crisps, sleeping and watching clever films I was staying out of trouble. Albeit I was barely leaving the house, or engaging with life, but at least I wasn't having the insane meltdowns, staying up for five days straight, causing chaos for myself and everyone around me, then having to deal with the emotional fallout. There were huge periods of my life where I think drugs saved me. When I couldn't cope with certain things going on in my life at the time, drugs got me through.

They sedated me and kept me docile.

And then when they stopped working, I'd simply change them up. Like musical chairs.

All I was doing was a terrible job at avoiding what I really needed to do.

I had an amazing therapist at the Margaret Centre. His name was Dominic and he was wonderfully supportive. Again, this was back in the days when not only could you get outstanding help for addiction, but also weekly therapy on the NHS without a long waiting list.

I saw Dominic for a couple of years, but my life was in such turmoil, and I was persistently missing appointments, that at some point I drifted away due to my unmanageability.

A few years later, at another rock bottom, I went in to self-refer to re-engage with both drug and mental health

RECOVERY – THE FIRST DAY

services, and I passed him in the reception. I was embarrassed and looked away. Shame can be a powerful deterrent. It can make you turn away from the people reaching out, people who are trying to help.

Dominic called me an hour later.

'Was that you I saw earlier? I don't know if you want to come back and see me. If not, it's fine, but I want you to know it's an option'.

So I went back. He gave me so much of his time and was a huge help in getting me to a point of addressing all the things I'd been avoiding.

Like most addicts, I'd made a series of bad decisions when I was using, and my past was coming back to bite me on the arse. I was now being evicted, which was the final, perhaps inevitable outcome of it all. I was in recovery, so thankfully I'd developed some coping skills, and these meant that I could deal with it all in a more constructive manner.

Nine

I seek professional help

ASSESSMENT

Your GP can assess you based on medical history, current units being consumed and risk factors that are unique to you. This will help them to determine the most appropriate individual treatment. They might advise a supervised alcohol detox, which can provide a safe environment for managing withdrawal symptoms. They might conclude that it's safe for you to begin your sobriety plan independently, or suggest a medically assisted detox if you need closer monitoring and support. These can sometimes be done in the community, nurse-led, or you might opt for a residential rehab-based detox.

Such treatments can be very expensive, and there's a minefield of snake-oil merchants out there who are only too happy to clear out your family silver, so do your research, and check sites like Facebook and Twitter/X for former residents' forums to get honest reviews. Anyone can write a TripAdvisor or Google review to say how wonderful a facility is. And make sure to read the reports by the regulatory body for health care facilities, the Care Quality Commission.

Having an open and honest conversation with your GP is not only a wise decision but is also an important first step towards a healthier life, free of alcoholism. It can provide you with the necessary tools, support you to navigate risks and set you up for successfully giving up. Just remember that you need to prioritise your health and well-being, and for the love of God don't take medical advice from anyone on social media who claims to be an expert, especially someone without a medical qualification in alcohol detoxes. There are so many of these charlatans about. Please be vigilant about this. It's your life on the line.

MAKE A PLAN

It's worth taking stock of your surroundings when you make the decision to get clean and sober, and establish a strong support system. One of the most effective strategies in early recovery is to thoroughly clear out from where you live all drug paraphernalia, all alcohol, and any items that could potentially trigger thoughts and cravings. This will contribute towards creating a healthier atmosphere at home, which can help to minimise temptation and to reinforce your commitment to getting and staying sober.

I SEEK PROFESSIONAL HELP

As well as clearing out your home environment, it's important to share your plan with your friends, family and overall support network, the ones who will have your back. Sharing this not only builds trust that might have been broken, but these people can begin to understand and support you in your commitment.

Their encouragement and affirmation can be invaluable.

JOIN A GROUP/GET HELP

Join support groups like Alcoholics Anonymous or Narcotics Anonymous, or your GP might be able to suggest other local groups. These can be in-person or virtual, and they can be incredibly beneficial.

These mutual aid groups can provide safe spaces where you can connect with others who are on similar journeys. Shared experiences, challenges and successes can help motivate you and build up your resilience.

Being surrounded by other people who understand where you're at can create a sense of belonging and accountability.

Making incremental changes to your environment can really motivate and set you up to give yourself a fighting chance to sustain abstinence, while at the same time laying the foundation for what can be an OK life.

EARLY DAYS

The first rung of the ladder will probably be one of the hardest and most painful experiences you'll face. You might have arrived at the decision of your own accord, been dragged kicking and screaming to a meeting or rehab by family or mates, or you may have been put in rehab by work, but one thing is apparent – you've realised you need genuine help. It's a pivotal moment, and perhaps you or your family have already reached out to drug and alcohol services to kick off the process. This time is crucial, and it's the beginning.

In your first week, depending on the substance you've been using, you might need some form of medical detox. It's up to you how easy or difficult a detox is going to be: some people will struggle because their bodies are kicking against the withdrawal, but some will lean into the process, understanding that in order to come out the other side they have to go through with it. You will find yourself with time on your hands, and filling that time can be unsettling. So find the meetings, find the people who go and tell them where you're at in the process, and they can suggest things to do and places to go in your area.

I SEEK PROFESSIONAL HELP

BE BRAVE

Withdrawal can be challenging and scary. It's what puts loads of people with the best intentions off ever getting clean and sober, but the alternative is so much worse in the long term.

You might experience nausea, sweating tremors, itching, insomnia and a few more besides – again this can depend on what you were using.

You might have psychological cravings, feel full of fear, anxiety and dread – unfortunately, these are all completely normal, they're shit, but they don't last forever.

The change of routine from using drugs and/or drinking daily and habitually is going to feel weird. Your routine previously may have consisted of getting up, rolling a spliff, draining the leftovers in the bottles and cans, or the half hour of bleariness before fixing up – we all have the things we did. Not doing this stuff will feel odd.

There will be a void and you'll need to find a healthy way to fill it.

If you aren't doing rehab and you're in your own house or wherever you live, you're going to have to make the changes previously suggested.

HAVE A CLEAR-OUT

Get rid of the drug paraphernalia, delete the numbers on your phone, and go through your messages and give your device a thorough detox. Block the numbers belonging to your dealers; if some of them don't hear from you for a while, they may contact you to check in, see how you are. I know this is a difficult thing to read and do, and like any relationship it's hard, but you're not in a romantic relationship with them. They're not your family, they don't give a shit about you and, sorry for the spoiler alert, they don't miss you. They miss your money.

If you can't do this for yourself, find someone who you know cares and ask them to help you. This will give you some accountability because you might want to keep a number just in case – it's risky, so try not to. Give yourself the best fighting chance at this.

A HIGHER POWER

If you've found your way to twelve-step meetings, try to go every day. Make it a priority. Get numbers of other members, call them. Some may not pick up immediately; they may be at work or doing stuff that's none of your business. Don't take it personally. Call another

I SEEK PROFESSIONAL HELP

number. Get the leaflets from the meetings and read them.

Don't be put off by the G word. Don't use the word 'God' as an excuse to shirk meetings. It's just a word; the programme was written a long time ago in the Bible Belt of America, it's just what it is. Some people take comfort in it, some don't. It's horses for courses.

You'll hear people talk about a higher power, and this might be alien to you. But put simply, it's just about trusting something bigger than you to help get you through.

Someone explained to me that in a situation like an accident in which you broke your leg, you wouldn't pray for your leg to heal, you'd go to a surgeon to fix it. In that instance, they're a higher power, because they could fix something you can't. My wife used nature as her higher power – she talked to the birds in her back garden. Enough said about that one.

Find the meetings near you or get the online meetings links from the relevant websites. It's going to be strange.

If you go out after work on a Friday, make your excuses to the crowd you go with and attend a meeting instead. They don't need to know if you choose not to tell them. If there are people going out for dinner or a coffee after the meeting, go with them. It's a good way of learning to live without using drugs and alcohol. The people you meet may not be the usual type of people you've been associating with – they'll be a mixed bag – but they'll give a shit about you and want to see you come back time and time again. They'll want you to succeed.

You can't be complacent about still going to the places where you once used. It's never advisable to return to the scene of a crime, so you're going to have to change it up.

NINETY DAYS

The recommended attendance is ninety meetings in ninety days, because it takes ninety days of doing something for it to become part of your lifestyle and for you to make the necessary changes. It sets you up with coping skills, better self-awareness and an invaluable support network. I've seen it being applied to quite a few things since coming into recovery, and it's been repurposed so many times as if it's an original idea – because it works. There's the 21/90 rule, for instance, which says it takes twenty-one days to make a habit and ninety days to make it part of your lifestyle.

Ninety in ninety sounds huge in your first week, but just take it day by day. Don't get overwhelmed early on in the process; every day you're doing this is a win, and the fact you started is excellent.

Try not to make any huge decisions; it'll be tempting to do so, but you're going to feel fragile and vulnerable. Don't expect to get well overnight. It's not a magic wand.

I SEEK PROFESSIONAL HELP

Wherever you are is where you need to be at most points.

You're going to have to accept that not everyone will be overjoyed at your newfound way of life. You'll possibly have people around you who are suspicious and sceptical. They may have had experiences of you where you've stolen, lied or let them down. But keep doing what you're doing. Actions speak louder than words.

You're not doing this for anyone apart from yourself, so all that stuff will fall into place later.

Don't rush it, it's not a race. It's one foot in front of the other and it's one day at a time

You'll possibly start to reassess things: your relationships, your job – if you've managed to hold onto it – and where you are in the world. You might look around you and think that everyone else knows what they're doing, but the reality is that they don't. Most people are just winging it. I used to sit in meetings and be astounded that people who'd started attending a few weeks before me could recite passages from the twelve-step literature. I'd sit there, beating myself up, thinking I wasn't the perfect recovering addict. I later realised that they just had bloody good recall and were great at remembering. It didn't mean they were the most super-spiritual recovering addicts, nor that I wasn't doing my best. I just had a shit memory.

You'll probably start noticing everyone else's drinking and using habits, and possibly even become evangelical about your new way of life. You might want to save these people from themselves, and tell them they have problems with alcohol and substances. This might very well be the case, but what they're doing is none of your business. Right now they're not your concern. This is about you and your own recovery, so try to focus on sorting yourself out first. You can address anything else later down the line.

You might be able to take time off work to adjust, as well as getting to appointments and meetings. Gauge your employer. You might have a sympathetic HR department, so you could maybe talk to them and see what provisions they can put in place. Perhaps you could get to a meeting during your lunch break or leave slightly earlier at the end of the day to get to one.

MIND YOUR SUGAR

Drink water, eat as healthily as you possibly can and watch your sugar intake – this is a difficult one, as sugar hits the same pleasure receptors as drugs and alcohol, so it's easy to fall into replacing one for the other, as harmless as it may seem. Get some sweets, but be mindful of the intake – there's a line in the twelve steps that says: 'One is too many, a thousand never enough.' This applies to jelly babies too.

★ ★ ★

I SEEK PROFESSIONAL HELP

Be gentle on yourself. This is not a race, it's a lifelong process that requires daily work, and it gets easier, it gets better and you get better.

And to quote the weird phrase they say at the end of meetings, it works if you work it, so work it – you're worth it.

Ten
Living with sobriety

Prior to recovery I didn't know anyone who didn't use drugs. This doesn't mean that all my friends and acquaintances were drug addicts, but everyone did drugs, whether it was just having a drink or smoking weed, or maybe cutting a few lines of coke on a Saturday night. Towards the end of my using, this circle shrank to just the heaviest users. We were like the survivors of a shipwreck, struggling to catch air.

Starting on the journey of recovery was like stepping into an entirely new realm. It transcended just stopping using drugs; it revolved around and relied upon the connection with other recovering addicts. This was where the magic lay. The type of friendships I made mirrored the intensity of those in my teenage years, and they were similar in the sense of their impact on me. There's an inexplicable connection that's forged when you have a shared experience, a form of trauma bonding, I suppose. It can be difficult to talk about this to others who haven't had the same experiences as a result of the carnage that drug use brings.

I couldn't share a meaningful conversation with someone who's climbed Mount Everest because I haven't had that experience. I could listen to what they have to say and be really interested, but there would be no common experience, no mutual identification.

In Narcotics Anonymous I found my tribe after years of being on the periphery.

The friends I made in recovery were diverse to say the least. In the early days you make very fast friends because you're seeing the same people regularly, but as you get a bit of time under your belt and life starts happening, you may not see them as regularly. Sadly, some don't always stick it out. There are conventions that happen up and down the country every couple of months, where all the lunatics descend on a hotel on the outskirts of a city and it's fun, a celebration of recovery! God help the poor unsuspecting normal guests; you can spot them by the look of sheer bafflement on their faces.

I have, however, made significant friendships of the type that will be lifelong, and these are the ones that have become more like family.

I met my wife in recovery. We met at one of those conventions.

I was at a point where I was four years sober, having lost my house and ended up living in a hostel with other addicts. It wasn't where I thought I'd end up, but my using had consequences, and homelessness was one of them.

LIVING WITH SOBRIETY

Up to that point I'd been in and out of relationships with other recovering addicts, all disastrous because of where I was in terms of my life. My first sober relationship was a revelation. She was Spanish, and initially she was renting a room in my house before we got together. It lasted as long as she was in the country. When she moved back to Spain I was distraught, a tough feeling to manage without being able to rely on the numbness that drugs gave me, but it was a pain I managed to get through. It showed me that I could manage my emotions, set boundaries and appreciate a relationship for what it was, a far cry from the relationships I'd had in the past. While I was using, my relationships were short-lived and tumultuous, a passionate six months of love bombing followed by a year of increasing chaos. I would become controlling, disappear for days at a time and then wonder why it all fell apart. I was always the victim of my own story. A combination of recovery and therapy helped me to confront my patterns; I saw how I was repeating the same behaviours that I hated in my parents.

Meeting my wife was a significant turning point in my life. She was three years sober and still working out the complexities of living in recovery. She had two boys and had managed to keep them safe and healthy through her active addiction. She had a chaotic warmth, bordering on being stark raving bonkers, and was incredibly practical. She lived in another city in a warm, disorganised home that at any time of the day would be filled with recovering addicts for whom she'd cook and make endless cups of tea. She was always in the kitchen. She had a loud French transgender lodger who was obsessed with superhero films and would watch them with the kids in the living room, a bright-purple front door and two mangy psycho cats called Cat and Other Cat.

What struck me was her lack of judgement about the situation I was in. She didn't give a toss that I lived in a hostel or that I was unemployed. We could talk about the times when we struggled in a way that didn't need explanation or justification. She had no judgemental attitude towards my past and no expectations that things were going to be perfect.

One of the earliest conversations we had was about my past behaviours and some of the things I'd done. I remember feeling vulnerable, afraid that she'd be horrified and ask me to leave. Instead she looked at me with her eyebrows raised – the same withering look my daughter now gives me when she thinks I'm being ridiculous – and said, 'No one chooses addiction. No one wakes up in the morning and thinks, "Oh, I know what I'll do. I'll smoke crack," like it's a lifestyle choice or a career move. Every single person in those cold church halls is there for a reason and no one came in with a polished halo. You're not that special – I've heard far worse.'

She set up NA meetings that provided childcare because at that point there wasn't any. She went to Sure Start and convinced them why it would be a good idea to provide support in the form of free crèche workers to help families to get clean of drugs in the community. She worked hard at her recovery, and helped any waif or stray that was on her radar, especially the mothers.

It was my first real experience of a family in recovery. I had no idea what I was doing, but I was welcomed and trusted. Her boys were three and thirteen at the time, and she was raising them alone, juggling their childcare. I offered to step in and help. I'd spend weekdays at her house and she'd come down to London when the boys went to their grandparents every other weekend. That's when I started to feel like I belonged in the world. I was trusted to look after this little kid with a funny accent and floppy hair who was obsessed with Spider-Man. It was easy, it was fun and I loved every minute of it – we were like a little gang. He's eighteen now, has a posh north London accent, still has the floppy hair and likes girls. We've had our own struggles with him over the years, but we have the benefit of being in recovery to help him work the big life stuff out and a safety net to catch him.

The thirteen-year-old is now twenty-eight and has grown up all his adult life with a mum who worked her way out of the mess she was in and is a great example of what recovery can retrieve. We have a fantastic relationship and he calls me with the stuff his mum will lose the plot over.

She got pregnant a few years after we first started seeing each other, and we decided to fully commit to the relationship. She decided that she'd up sticks and move down to London, as she only lived where she did because of previous circumstances. She'd lived in London years before and was ready to go back. We got a flat through bidding from the council (I was entitled to bid due to living in a hostel). It was big enough for three people at best, and we threw ourselves into decorating it from the floorboards up. My mate Charlie was a great help with this because I didn't have the first clue about decorating. At one point I had three grown men in my flat, all with paintbrushes in their hands, all in recovery. Honestly, it was like being in a Marx Brothers film – utter madness – but we got the flat finished and it was beautiful, all done by people with varying degrees of time in recovery. I'm incredibly lucky to have these people in my life, and it was one of those examples of the saying, 'It takes a village to raise a child,' which I totally understood after that.

The whole situation was terrifying and exhilarating at the same time. Not long before I was incapable of looking after myself, and here I was, a responsible adult, one that took care of teeny-tiny humans.

It forced me to grow up a bit and think beyond myself. My love for my wife was initially about how she made me feel. With my daughter it was different; she was the first person whose needs I put before my own without harbouring feelings of resentment and begrudgery.

LIVING WITH SOBRIETY

Being a dad gave me an actual purpose that I'd never experienced before. It doesn't have to be kids, it just has to be bigger than yourself, something that gives your life meaning. It might be your career, a pet or a cause, anything that doesn't revolve around you, but for me it was my daughter.

I mentioned earlier that I didn't have children during my addiction, as I was careful about not wanting to pass my chaos onto another generation. I didn't want my children to hate or resent me in the same way I did my own parents. It was one of the only responsible decisions I made during that time.

In twelve-step recovery meetings they'd talk about a life beyond your wildest dreams. I thought I'd already done that – touring with Oasis, doing drugs with models. I was really insecure and unsure of myself, so I thought that stuff meant something and I mattered because I'd hung out with X, Y or Z. Looking back on it now makes me realise how hollow and superficial it all was; my wildest dream was something I didn't realise even existed when I was surrounded by sycophants and liggers, and that is hanging out with my daughter – and she likes hanging out with me. None of that other stuff matters anymore. It's funny how your perceptions of what's fun can change if you allow yourself to drop the mask.

Recovery teaches me that life isn't about comfort. Before, if something didn't suit me, serve me or didn't feel good, I didn't bother. Over the years I came to realise that discomfort is part of the package. Strangely, I still like it sometimes. I feel everything now: panic, anxiety, guilt, shame, the lot. I learned the hard way that life shows up warts and all – you've got to take the bad as well as the good – and I've signed up for the lot. It's so different from all the years I was just existing, hiding behind using drugs. I wouldn't even notice things like huge events, like friends having babies. I'd see them in the street with a buggy and would wonder when that happened. Life goes on while you're standing still, frozen in time. But no more!

Ironically, the more I grew in my recovery, the more I was drawn back to where I grew up, like an instinctual homing pigeon. But years afterward, in 2013, I was walking from a meeting in Camden and realised that I knew no one. I hadn't stopped to talk to anyone in thirty minutes. It was odd, the first time I'd ever felt like a stranger in my own neighbourhood.

My grandparents and great-grandparents are from the area, and I have documents dating back to the Great War linking us to the area. My mum worked in youth services, was part of setting up City Farm and did a stint at the *Camden New Journal*, while both my parents helped created the skate bowl in Talacre Park. The place is in my blood. Now I don't know anyone there and everything had changed; no one who I know who grew up there can afford to live in the area, and they've been replaced by a different class. Every pub, every shop front had a story attached, but the people were long gone, victims of social cleansing. I was home, but it wasn't my home anymore, and I wondered what I was clinging to.

My wife was pregnant at the time, and we quickly realised that the flat we'd put so much effort into was not going to be fit for purpose. I was trying to swap with a flat or house in Camden or Kentish Town, hoping to bring the baby up there. When the realisation hit me that it was never going to be the same as it used to be, I gave up looking there. This was much to the relief of my wife, who didn't want to live there. She can do an hour in Camden before she wants to get away.

We got lucky, really lucky, ending up with a house in Crouch End. I wasn't too familiar with the area, but my wife's family had lived there since the 60s and 70s, so we were bloody delighted. The move marked a new chapter.

Crouch End has its own community, and after a while I started to feel at home. At first I couldn't see why the change would be beneficial, but because the place had no connection to my past, it was a fresh beginning with my new family to start making my own memories, ones that didn't have any bittersweet connotations. I was rebuilding my life, and I came to realise that home wasn't just a place, but the people you surround yourself with. The place I grew up in will always be a part of me, but my family home is where I'm growing and becoming the person I want to be.

Having kids with no family support wasn't easy. My wife is Irish, but most of her family – as big as it was – had moved out of London. I was a fish out of water, but luckily she had the experience of raising two children on her own, so it wasn't as hard on her. I was fourteen years into an epic strop with my mum, and obviously my dad …

He doesn't know my family. He tries in his own way, but it's too fractured … and he's too fractured. I don't take the kids around to his as the place is a state, a living testament to his fragility and his refusal to acknowledge his issues.

Even the one time he did help, it ended up with the police being involved because my daughter kicked off. I'd left him for a short time with her, and because they were so unfamiliar with each other someone called the police because they thought he'd snatched her and was managing the situation badly.

I had to rush back and show the police Facebook photos on my phone to prove she was my daughter. It was a sad example of how detached and fractious the whole relationship was.

Building a family in recovery has been both challenging and rewarding, one of the greatest yet scariest experiences of my life. It has made me confront my fears and my shortcomings, but also helped me appreciate my skills and strengths in ways I never thought possible.

LIVING WITH SOBRIETY

Every day I try to be the best version of myself for my family, and not the man who was plagued by generational trauma and dysfunction. I'm working hard to break the cycle that plagued my family before me.

Don't get me wrong, I don't always get it right. I'm still capable of being a lazy, disorganised fuck-up, but I'm aware of my defects now, which is huge growth.

My relationship with my mum was always tricky and messy. In my twenties we had a row over something trivial and didn't speak for fourteen years. It was an argument about my brother – his increasing drug use and deteriorating mental health. It could have been resolved, but stubbornness runs through my family and coupled with an inability to communicate effectively and honestly, it just went on unchecked.

Towards the end of my wife's pregnancy she started to voice some concern that my mum didn't know and how unfair it was. She didn't want to be walking down the street and bump into her years later, and have to introduce her to a grandchild she knew nothing about. Despite my relationship with her, she felt it was important for Mum to know she had a grandchild.

I didn't have a contact number for her, so I relied on my dad to tell her. They had been separated for a long time but still had contact because of my brother's condition. Dad dragged his heels for months in some weird idiotic attempt to control the situation. I'll never know to this day his reasons for not telling her or giving me her phone number.

We even bumped into my brother, and when he mentioned to my dad that my wife looked different, he said that she'd gotten fat – not a mention that she was pregnant.

Although my dad is now in his 70s, he's still very emotionally immature, still with no sense of awareness or responsibility. He blames me, my mum – whom he hadn't been with for almost thirty years – and my brother for his shitty life. Two of the people he blames are dead, but he still talks about how everything that is wrong in his life is our fault. He blames women and children rather than taking a look at his problems and seeing that he had a part in them.

I seemed to have inherited that knack!

Dolly came into the world early on a Friday morning in April. She was pink and squishy and looked perplexed. Her eyes were open and bright.

She was born onto an Arsenal towel to a George Clinton soundtrack, albeit drowned out by my wife's expletives. The birth was complicated due to her shoulder being lodged in the birth canal. I was so freaked out that I almost threw up. Thankfully we live in a progressive country where we have highly skilled midwives to whom this stuff is a daily occurrence and who can sort it out with a few manoeuvres. Hello, Dolly!

LIVING WITH SOBRIETY

Two weeks later, and after five months of badgering him for my mum's number, Dad finally got round to telling my mum about the baby. He said she wanted a picture. I thought, *OK, I can manage that.*

Like everything I overthought it; I was structuring an image of my family portrait in my head. Should it be tongue in cheek, something that will make her laugh? Or should it be formal? What should we wear? I decided that after having had no contact for fourteen years, the best thing to do was to send a normal candid family photo.

That night I found myself wide awake, mulling over what the relationship was going to look like. If we couldn't straighten our differences out, would she still have a relationship with her grandchildren? How would that all work? Would we do Sunday dinners, or would she be an arm's-length grandparent who sends a tenner in the post at Christmas?

The next morning, 9 a.m. on the dot, my phone rang. It was my father.

'Your mother's dead.'

He said those words with no emotion, flat as a pancake. No build-up, no 'Are you sitting down?' or 'Are you on your own?' Nothing.

He lives ten minutes away on the overground, but he couldn't be bothered to come to tell me face to face.

At fifty-eight, my mum died of a drug-induced heart attack. She had never touched drugs when I was a child –

neither of my parents did, though my father is so uptight I do wonder if it might have benefited him – but my brother had gotten her into legal highs a few years earlier.

She was living alone in Wales; she had lost one son to a psychiatric ward and was estranged from the other. Loneliness was worse for her heart than depression, fags and a bad diet. The sad irony was that she had spent years worrying about my brother's drug use, and in the end her own experimentation ended her life.

My daughter was two weeks old, and on top of the exhaustion and overwhelming love I felt, I was hit with some new emotions – rage and this gnawing sense of regret. Rage at my father, and the regret of not acting sooner and being more proactive with my mother.

Was it worth it, fourteen years of silence? What was the bloody point? All that time wasted, the potential memories never made, and I was sitting there with a grandchild she'd never meet and a chance at reconciliation lost forever.

After that call I sat on the edge of my bed, Dolly in my arms. She was so tiny and warm. I held on to her with the resolve that I would be the best father. I whispered to her that I'd do better, that I'd be the dad she deserved. It was a stark contrast to what I'd have done if I was still using drugs. I probably would have used that as a prime excuse to go missing on a bender, drowning my sorrows and not facing anything head-on.

LIVING WITH SOBRIETY

But instead I looked at this new life in my arms, a stark contrast to the death that I'd just learned about.

It was almost as if the universe said: Here's your chance to do something different. Don't fuck it up.

Mum's funeral was in Mid Wales, which on public transport may as well have been the edge of the world. My wife's mum, who was living in Spain, drove all the way over to make sure we got there with no stress. Another example of recovery: my wife and her mum had only just recently reconciled after a stupid argument.

The service was very impersonal. A priest who had probably never met my mum spouted platitudes about how wonderful she was. My brother was strung out, hood up, and I'm not sure he even knew where he was or why he was there. My father hung his head with shame. Mum had a few friends who spoke with me afterwards, all with really lovely things to say. At the time the words didn't go in, but my wife and her mum listened because they knew they'd repeat them to me later when I wasn't so shell-shocked.

As painful as it was going through that process, it felt good in terms of where I was in my life. I was now equipped to deal with stuff without resorting to using. Experiencing those moments of pain that I'd rather be few and far between made me appreciate the good stuff. I stopped taking drugs to be involved with life, the whole spectrum, and that included the bits I'd previously have rather erased and blocked out.

Grief is an odd one, as it's certainly not linear. It hits you when you least expect it. It sneaks in when you're not looking and wallops you. Then I'm back at the moment when I picked the phone up to hear my father's voice telling me she was gone. The futility of it sometimes is hard to deal with.

Then there's the guilt. Not just about the years of silence, but what came after. After a few years Dolly started asking questions about where my mummy was. I didn't know how to have that grown-up conversation, and I didn't know how to explain death to a child, so I told her she lived in Wales. As soon as I'd said it, I knew I was trapped in a lie. This went on until Dolly was five years old. I didn't know at what point I could be honest with her and tell her the truth. I didn't even want to say out loud that my mum didn't exist anymore.

Change is never easy, especially when you've grown up in a family where honest conversations were as rare as hens' teeth. We never talked about the big, important elephant-in-the-room stuff, we just swept it under the carpet like any normal dysfunctional family does. Pretended everything was OK. My parents' marriage fell apart and the lead-up was ignored until one day my mum wasn't there anymore.

When my brother was struggling with addiction and mental health issues, they acted like it wasn't happening. And here I was repeating the same behaviours with my little girl.

LIVING WITH SOBRIETY

That lie is one of my biggest regrets. I lied to myself: I told myself that I was trying to protect her, but really I was just protecting myself from having to deal with the death of my mum and having a difficult conversation with my daughter. It taught me about the importance of transparency and honesty, even when stuff is difficult. It also taught me that I'm raising my children to be resilient and that they can handle way more than I'm protecting them from or give them credit for. And the bottom line is that they deserved the truth.

One day I was rummaging through old boxes I had in storage – I'm known to hoard stuff, although I prefer the term 'collect' – and I found an old photo of my mum holding me as a baby. Her face was lit up with joy, her eyes full of love, the expressions you can't fake. It was nothing like the image I'd had of her for years. People are complicated, and my mum was more than just our arguments and silences. She was a person with her own battles and pain. In that moment, frozen in time, I saw the woman I'd been angry with for such a long time. She was a mum filled with hope, looking at her baby like I looked at my baby, with all the love I had in me.

I keep that photo next to my bed; it reminds me how far I've come in learning to forgive. Not just my mum, but myself too. I'm learning to let go, to stop dragging around the baggage of my life, all the guilt and regret. Some days are easier than others. Some days I want to hide the photo in a drawer because the grief creeps in. But there on my bedside table it stays as a reminder of the complexities of family and the importance of forgiveness.

I tell Dolly about her gran, all the really cool stuff she did, how she was a hard worker and how much I respect her for that. How she gave me a love of books, and how people thought we were posh because we had books. This makes her laugh, but it's true!

I try to focus on the positive, leaving the arguments and the years of estrangement out. Maybe when she's older we'll have that conversation, but for now I want her to have a good image of the grandmother she'll never know. I feel a sadness about that. But all we have is the here and now.

I suppose what I'm going the long way about saying is that I try to forgive myself for not knowing better, for giving away my power, for all my past behaviours, the survival patterns and traits I picked up while growing up, and for being a twat. It doesn't come easy; I'm harder on myself than anyone ever has been on me. You might also find this to be the case with yourself.

But it's a process, one of many you find in recovery, the ones that teach us that recovery is not just about staying sober, it's about fixing all the parts of your life that you thought were beyond repair. It can be hard work. In some respects it can be harder than actually coming off drugs because it isn't just about not doing something, it's about actively working on yourself, day in, day out.

LIVING WITH SOBRIETY

Part of that work is learning to be honest. After a lifetime of being dishonest, this can be a hard habit to break because honesty can feel uncomfortable. It's breaking the silence and secrecy, and shining a big light on everything. Secrets shrivel up and die in the light. It might hurt a bit to start, but it's the only way to truly begin to heal the past.

One of the last times I saw my brother was when I almost walked past him in the street. He was barely recognisable, but as he got closer I knew it was him. He looked rough, and was so overweight from the antipsychotics he was on for schizophrenia that it was like looking at his reflection in a funhouse mirror. At the time I was walking down Oxford Street with some friends after a gig at Hyde Park on our way home, but very few of even my closest friends had ever met him. It was the first time in ages that I'd seen him outside of a hospital ward as he'd been in and out of institutions for at least twelve years.

He casually asked how I was, and we exchanged a few words before he said he had to get off. And that was it, a sibling relationship of shared childhood histories reduced to a few awkward pleasantries on the street. We both walked off in opposite directions, like we always seemed to do in life. One of my major regrets is not making more of an effort with my brother, but I had a complicated relationship with him.

He was profoundly unwell and clearly in need of help, a lot more than he was getting. I was running the Secret

Drug Addict, helping strangers on the internet, and yet I couldn't reach my own brother. It's sometimes easier to help a stranger than to get embroiled with the messy, complicated emotions that come with family members.

To really get better, people need to want to help themselves, but sometimes the most help you can give them is just being with them, giving them your time. Sometimes giving help doesn't mean helping someone to feel better, it can mean just helping someone feel less lonely on their journey through life, wherever it's taking them. Being a presence, a constant in their life, like a north star in their chaos.

I think about all the times I could have reached him, made more of an effort. Called him more, visited him more, the smallest of gestures that might have made a difference. But I didn't, and I'll live with and wrestle with that for the rest of my life.

After my brother had walked off, one of my friends piped up and asked whether I knew him. To them he looked like just another street junkie, which is what he'd become, I suppose. But this street junkie was my baby brother.

So I nodded and said yes, I know him, and we carried on.

I wish I'd had the courage to turn back, to try to bridge the gap between us. It haunts me, keeps me awake at night, wondering what if I'd encouraged him to carry on the conversation properly, made an effort to arrange to meet him regularly. He might not have beaten his drug addiction, but he might have been less lonely, his ending less miserable and untimely.

I'd been an only child up to the age of nine, and I was delighted when he was born. But we didn't really grow up together, not properly. He was only four when my mum left for the women's refuge, and he was there with her until he was eleven. He may as well have been on another planet for all we saw of each other, and by the time she brought him back to London I was deep in my own addiction and he promptly started going off the rails ...

I didn't know it at the time, but he would be out until all hours with his mates, getting off his face. He was expelled from school and packed off to a boarding school for kids with complex needs – he was dyslexic as well – in Brighton. He didn't last long. He was expelled for flooding the toilets and that was that, his education done and dusted at fifteen, with not a single GCSE between us. He lasted at school longer than I did, but only just.

There was always drama with him, some crisis; he was crying out for attention and love, but they were never forthcoming. Drugs were his way of coping. And where was his big brother? Off my face, descending into my own madness, too much of a selfish prick to give him a second thought, too busy creating my own dramas to be present for him. He did come to stay with me for a time, and was already showing signs of being seriously unwell from all the weed he was smoking. I was twenty-three, trying to be a figure of authority for him and getting it all wrong. It was a disaster.

He ended up back at my dad's and we drifted apart. We were never close after that. He developed drug-induced schizophrenia at the age of fifteen. That's the first time he was sectioned. His life was derailed before he could even get started living. We smoked as much weed as each other, but I seem to have dodged that genetic defect by luck. It astounds me that when there's so much talk of mental health awareness weeks, well-being forums and all the rest of it, the fact that our society is a pressure cooker for the creation of mental illness is not being looked at holistically at a grassroots level.

There are children in this country living in abject poverty, going to school hungry, eating ultra-processed foods and they can't focus. Parents are working every hour God sends them to keep a roof over their heads, so as a result of time poverty these children aren't being nurtured. Instead they're being parented by online apps and games. There are no youth services left and after-school groups are extortionately expensive. Dolly does ballet, swimming, gymnastics and craft club. I work to pay for her extracurricular activities. If I was a single-parent family on a low wage I'd be fucked, and my kids would have had their own keys at age five. We had excellent youth services run by amazing and inspiring people when I was a kid, but that's now all a distant memory. We are setting these kids up to fail on every rung of the ladder. And then we wonder why they turn to drugs and other rubbish behaviours to help them cope.

It's about dodging pain and the drugs help. To begin with, at least.

When my brother was first admitted to hospital, the psychiatrist told my parents that under no circumstance should he smoke any weed. They were crystal-clear about that. He was hearing voices and smoking weed would exacerbate this. What they didn't say was don't let him smoke crack, heroin, take benzos and alcohol. Just keep him off the weed.

Drug addicts can be pestering, annoying nuisances, and people around them want a quiet life, so my brother was left to his own devices. There was not much any of us could do, despite the begging and pleading with him and those around him.

By his twenties my brother was a mess. Covered in tattoos, wandering the streets in tracksuit bottoms, shirtless, with a psycho dog by his side. He was not a tough kid, he was petrified. He had no friends, no life, never had a job, and the girlfriend he was with for a short time was as unwell as he was. But mainly it was just him and the voices in his head.

Once he started on crack and heroin, his life became a revolving door of arrests and prison. He had about seventy arrests in total, all drug-related, the common denominator that was ignored over and over, time and time again. He'd be sectioned for twenty-eight days and they'd stick him on another form of medication. He'd eat, sleep and start to look human again, but then once that time was up, they'd release him back out onto the streets, and he'd go to pieces. He'd stop taking his antipsychotics, stop eating, stay up for days on end getting wasted and fall apart all over again. I can't blame him, if I'm honest. The medication he was on had some nasty side-effects. He'd blow up like a balloon and he said it made him feel like a zombie, with no will to do anything. His existence consisted of being off his head with illegal or prescription drugs, neither being ideal.

When Covid hit he was placed in the psychiatric unit at the Whittington Hospital, where he was locked up for ages. My dad couldn't visit, so I'd drop vapes and bits off to him once a week. He was then moved to the psych unit at St Pancras Hospital, where he lived for almost three years.

Finally, they placed him in some hostel in Camden, an under-resourced, skeletal service, badly run by mainly agency and bank staff who did not give a stuff or were in any way experienced enough to deal with the residents' complex issues.

Six weeks later he was found dead in his room. Overdosed.

He hadn't used street drugs for a while, so his tolerance had dropped off. My brother Sam was thirty-six. I beat

LIVING WITH SOBRIETY

myself up wondering if I could have done more, or done anything different. But I couldn't have him at the house with the children, not in the state that he was in.

The last time I heard from him was over Facebook. He messaged me after I'd posted a photo of Kim Gordon. My brother wasn't into music – he was too consumed by drugs from a young age – but for me drugs and music went hand in hand. He was a different type of drug user. They dragged him away from life.

He asked me who she was. I told him she was the singer from Sonic Youth. He asked if I knew the New York Dolls. I replied that I did. And that was it. Our last chat.

Not long after that he was gone.

My dad broke the news in his usual fashion, over the phone in his monotonous, emotionless tone. My wife was at work and I was at home with the children. I called my wife and sobbed down the phone.

I know it was a Tuesday because I play football on a Tuesday. I love playing – it's my time. There's something pure about it: running around, kicking a ball, not thinking of anything much. It was one of the few things I did all throughout my using that wasn't utterly self-destructive. Now I'm getting on a bit and I'm more prone to injuries. When I was using I couldn't hold down a job or keep a girlfriend, but no matter how bad things got I always showed up for football.

Give me a ball and a yard of grass and I'm happy.

I texted Charlie, the guy who runs the game, and told him what had happened. I said that I was coming and I'd play, but if anyone started moaning about not passing or missing goals, I might punch someone.

There were nine people at my brother's funeral: my family, my father, my friend Matthew and a few kids who were friends with Sam who grew up on our street. We didn't know if he had any friends as an adult and had no way of contacting them. It was snowing heavily outside and we were huddled inside the crematorium, the hearse barely making it on account of the snow. Matthew spoke, which was very kind of him, and it was a touching moment when we remembered him before it all went so badly wrong. It felt like the only genuine moment in the whole sorry affair. I was incredibly grateful for that.

It would have felt wrong to listen to a priest or a stranger standing up talking about what a wonderful sense of humour he had or some other empty words. It would have made me furious. I find the lies condescending and impersonal, but I couldn't speak and my father couldn't bring himself to either. I refused any form of religious music, choosing to blast out the New York Dolls instead, which angered my father. I played it because it was the last thing we talked about. I don't even know if he really liked them. But it was a way of expressing something, how sad it made me and how I was sorry I didn't make more of an effort, that I didn't really know him and that he never really knew his big brother. It just couldn't have been sadder. If you typed what does a drug addict's funeral look like into a search engine, this is what it would show you.

Addicts die alone. They die young. They run out of friends. It's an incredibly sad existence. Their funerals are sparsely attended, and they cease to exist. No one talking about them, no one talking about what an amazing impact they had on their lives and what a great loss it is.

The only comfort I can take from it is that my baby brother is free of his suffering, because I could honestly not see a way out for him.

Addiction and severe mental health illness damage relationships, leaving the individual with fractured and transient relationships without any real lasting connections.

It feels sometimes people will champion mental health and wear it as a badge of honour, as something to talk and post about on Instagram, while not really understanding the complexities of real mental unwellness. I saw a video on TikTok a while back: a clean-cut kid, no more than twenty-five, was lying on the ground with a placard that said, *I am having a bad mental health day, I need a hug*. So all these people queued up to give him a hug. It was sweet and well meaning, but if John – the guy down the road who shouts at pedestrians and children, walks into oncoming traffic and sometimes forgets to get dressed – did the same, I doubt he'd get the same reaction. I know

I'd be reluctant to give him a hug, but I bet he needs one badly.

People need people to stand by them at their very worst, but that's hard when people are consumed by life. It's just how society is. I've met so many people like my brother, people who were lost, scared and searching for a way out. Some made it, some didn't. Every single one of those people taught me something different, about community and love.

We scattered my mum's ashes on a beach on the Isle of Wight, her favourite spot. I'll take Sam there soon.

These, I suppose, are incidents from a life lived in sobriety, the sort of stuff that in the past I thought I'd never be able to get through without using drugs or alcohol to numb and avoid the responsibility and pain.

I sometimes wonder about relapse. In my experience people relapse because they become complacent or they can't face the reality of their situation. They can't accept they're an addict or what it really means. I think once I got my head around what I was and accepted it, I sort of knew that I couldn't use safely. It wasn't about dying; it was more about not being able to control it. If I could control my drug use I'd only do it at the weekends; I wouldn't touch them during the week. I can't guarantee that, and to be honest I don't know if I'd really bother anymore. There's a peace that comes with surrender and accepting what I am. I like waking up on a Sunday morning in my own bed,

LIVING WITH SOBRIETY

knowing I didn't upset anyone the night before, not causing any drama. I like not having a hangover or a comedown. And I'm eighteen years older than I was when I stopped. I can't imagine how horrific a hangover would feel now.

Every time someone reaches out to me through the Secret Drug Addict, I think of my brother. I think of all the people out there who don't have someone to reach out to, who are fighting their battles alone. And I promise myself that I'll do better, that I'll be there for the next person who needs help, even if I failed to be there for my own brother when he needed me the most.

Because in the end, that's what recovery is all about. It's about learning from our mistakes, about doing better today than we did yesterday. It's about reaching out a hand to those who are still struggling, even when – especially when – it's hard.

I can't get extreme about anything because I struggle to manage it. To help explain this, just the other day I was running for the bus. I can see the bus stop and the bus is there. And just as I get to it, the bus pulls out and drives off. In that moment I feel a huge level of anger towards the bus and the bus driver, together with a sheer compulsion to punch someone's lights out. Even though I know that the next bus is going to be here in the next seven … eight … ten minutes, I still can't shake off my anger. The point is that there isn't one major thing that could throw you off balance. I won't sit here and tell you that a New Year's Eve party won't be difficult in the same way that missing the bus won't make you angry. The truth is that anything can be a trigger and it really is your state of mind and acceptance that life is happening whether you like it or not.

During lockdown some people found it easy not to drink because they didn't feel like they were missing out, but others drank a lot more than they would normally have done. There's no right or wrong answer, but if you're struggling with upcoming events and the fear of staying sober through them – here are some things that might help.

Eleven

Christmas Eve, New Year's Eve

FINDING JOY – WHAT BRINGS YOU JOY

Joy – what does it mean? It's very subjective, that's the first thing I'll say about it. It's not about what I enjoy doing, and what I find fun. If you don't see tangible improvements in your life, then progress, change.

For example, I am doing drugs and I am miserable. But then I stop doing drugs and I am still miserable. At least when I am doing drugs (and again I mean any type of drug that you may be addicted to) there is familiarity with the drug-taking misery. I am somehow more comfortable I'm that.

Like I often say, the worst part about addiction is that it's so intimate to you. It becomes your personality – so that leaving it all behind and changing can sometimes feel like killing a big part of who you are. The end result is that you don't know who you are in this new skin.

Change is quite hard to do, so why should I make the effort?

If I don't see things getting better then I might as well go back to what I know. I've been sober since 2007, so I can say with some certainty I won't go back to using, but it illustrates the situation most addicts find themselves in. Not even just addicts. Anyone that's tried to break a habit. The comfort you feel in carrying on as you are is far greater and far more appealing than the effort that it takes to make meaningful change.

This is where finding joy comes in. The things we take for granted are a good point. A lot of the things that do make me feel happy now are: watching the football in my house, going out to the café with a book (by the way I'll never enjoy taking the dog out for a walk), sitting and listening to music with my daughter where I can tell her about the bands and why I think they're great, and watching her reaction to it. And the biggest joy I find is when I hear her on her own listening to music in her room.

Life shouldn't be an extreme of ups and downs – the duller my life appears, the happier I am. The closer I get to a flat line of emotions, the more I know I am OK. What I mean is that I'm neither too happy nor too sad – a flat line for me is when things aren't brilliant nor a disaster. I guess it's when you can say: I'm good, not too bad, I'm all right.

So you have to find this balance, this joy in a boring, seemingly mundane life. You've got to accept that it can't be an all-day, all-night party with your best mates all the time, and that the joy of waking up sober beats one night out. As you embark on this journey to find the joy in your everyday life, it's essential that you look after your physical as well as your mental state. Getting enough sleep, eating healthily and exercising regularly are some of the most common ways of doing this, but you should also look to re-engage in activities that you've forgotten you like doing.

You used to play tennis when you were younger? Find a local club and join them for a session. Chances are you'll meet other people who like tennis and you'll be able to join them for another game. You may decide not to join a club straight away, but by re-engaging with something once you have a really good chance of finding someone who is as passionate as you are about that thing.

Filling the void with joy is absolutely key. When you're used to hanging out with the same people, drinking together for five hours or taking drugs for six hours every day for many years, and then you finally stop, you'll have a lot of time per day to fill that void. So whatever that might mean for you – what were you into before the drugs? Cinema? Cooking? Drawing? Playing tennis (see above), or perhaps you were really good at singing? It's important to engage with something that you used to do – something practical that you can do.

What are the things that bring you joy?

- Hitting a forehand
- Painting
- … ?

MY JOY LIST

1. _____
2. _____
3. _____
4. _____
5. _____

GRATITUDE LIST

When I'm talking to people, a gratitude list is one of the top things that come up. This is because I think that a lot of the time people focus on the negatives, and we all know that it can always be worse. We know we take a lot of things for granted, such as health and housing, and we do have the right to these things, but the reality is that some people die of cancer and other people may lose their house. You don't really have the right to anything – especially in this country. Even if you've lost your house, you still have options; you may be homeless, but you can have access to the hostel. What I'm trying to say is that there's always something to be grateful for, whatever the circumstances. Your dog dies, that's life, you feel sad, you get resentful; but if you write a gratitude list you can start to reflect on the joy and the happy years you spent together. These are some very basic examples but I think you get the point.

It's about finding that gratitude in the privilege that you have.

I should be grateful for another sober day, but the reality is that I sometimes take such an important thing as my sobriety for granted. There are those moments when I don't, but for me every day is just another day as it is for anyone else, with the same dread of having to go to work, and so on. So yes, writing a gratitude list regularly should be treated in the same way you would having a shower or making dinner. It should be an essential part of your life, not just something you do when you're feeling vulnerable or low. Similarly, it's important to keep doing it even when things are going great.

So yes, writing a gratitude list is something I do. It might be a good start and help you if you do so too. I'm going to take time out here and let you write your list of five things. My list is this and it will be fairly obvious:

- My daughter – she's a rock star
- My health, bad back and ankles aside, touch wood I am going well
- The roof over my head

Your turn. What's yours?

MY GRATITUDE LIST

1. _____
2. _____
3. _____
4. _____
5. _____

LOVE AND RELATIONSHIPS

If you managed to achieve some time in sobriety and held on to your existing relationship, you might have a sense of relief and hope. However, it's essential to recognise that while you've changed, the journey to rebuilding your relationship is just beginning and there will be a lot of time to make up for and amends to make. You might expect your partner to be brimming with joy and support for you. You're a changed person after all. Surely you should be receiving affirmation and praise for doing such a wonderful job, but that would be to forget all the hurt and upset you have caused for however long you've been using destructively. This is not going to go away overnight.

CHRISTMAS EVE, NEW YEAR'S EVE

Just like you are in recovery, your wife, husband or partner – if you have one – are also going through a form of recovery.

The trust might not come back for a very long time and they may be slow to forgive. They might be carrying a lot of anger and resentment that has been suppressed for a long time, so it's important to understand that the pain and hurt you caused during your period of destructive behaviour won't instantly disappear. The best thing you can do is keep putting the work in daily. In this case, actions do speak louder than words, and patience and understanding will be required.

If you've gotten sober and you didn't have a relationship to speak of before, this will be something you might think about.

It's never a good idea to rush into a relationship, as you will have work to do on yourself. There's a saying that you should first get a plant, see if you can keep that alive, then get a pet, same story, and if you can manage to keep both alive, then you're maybe ready for a relationship. Before getting involved in a relationship it's crucial to understand the potentially unhealthy dependence you might develop. Love produces the same chemicals – oxytocin, dopamine – as some of the drugs you might have been using. The neurochemicals can provoke a sense of euphoria. If you're in early recovery you might not be able to distinguish these feelings, and they can be intense. And just like the comedown from drugs can be devastating, so too can the relationship problems you're not equipped to deal with.

I can't say I did all the stuff that I was advised to do and avoid all the situations I got myself into. As a result, I ended up in a world of pain and caused a world of pain. But if I was to go back, I'd like to think I could adhere to the suggestions I was given. Who knows?

When you haven't given yourself the chance to recover and do some work on getting yourself emotionally stable, you might mistake love for obsession and control. The feelings are intense and hard to manage without the tools and experience of being in an adult relationship. If you're struggling to learn to love yourself, you're possibly going to struggle loving anyone else in a healthy way. It takes time to build up your self-esteem and self-worth, and the chances are that the types of relationships you'll find yourself in will be with the same sort of person as yourself. Finding sobriety is really a good opportunity to give yourself a break, take stock of all the debris and start to rebuild a life for yourself. I'm by no means suggesting a life of pious chastity, but take a breath. How can you love someone if you can't love yourself?

CHRISTMAS EVE, NEW YEAR'S EVE

FAMILY

These can be the most supportive and yet the trickiest relationships to navigate and manage. After all, they may well have installed the buttons. You might be estranged from them as a result of your behaviours, or they might be still in your life. They might have been the root cause of your behaviours, your biggest enablers, they might be your triggers or your biggest cheerleaders. Whatever the case is, it's a long process.

For example, my family were my biggest triggers and enablers by proxy. By being complacent with their parenting, they allowed me to take charge of my own life from a very young age and the results were disastrous for me, as I didn't know my arse from my elbow.

Some of the people I've spoken to come from families who were rigid in their rules growing up, so their addiction began as an act of rebellion; that's before it got so big it ceased to be rebellion and ended up a crippling hindrance. Family can attempt to solve your problems, and this can cause resentment, anger and frustration. You might not see your problem and how it's affecting them. They can lose their temper, lecture, plead, use barbed comments, not believe your promises because they've heard them all before, not trust you in their house because you've damaged their property or stolen it.

You might be desperate to prove yourself and become frustrated that they don't believe you. But like the relationship you might have with a partner, this will maybe not happen overnight. The hope is that they will want you to succeed and support you, but try not to be disappointed if that comes slowly.

You could perhaps let them into your new life. If you've chosen to go to meetings as a way of getting well, introduce the new people you've met to your family; let them see that it's working for other people and that it might possibly work for you too. You have a responsibility in the situation to help alleviate your family's anxiety.

There are specific family groups they can access. Let them know that they may need a place to process the effect you've had on them, and that there are other families in the same situation. Addiction is a family illness. One person may use, but the entire family suffers. Recovery is a collective process, and when that member of the family gets sober the benefits can be immense.

FRIENDSHIPS

Your friends might not understand what's going on, although they might well do if you were to fall down blackout drunk seven days a week. It could be that they hadn't noticed you'd come apart at the seams. Alternatively, they might have been supporting you when your family

CHRISTMAS EVE, NEW YEAR'S EVE

gave up the ghost, and have been pushed to the limits of what's acceptable. When I got into recovery, I started seeing my old pals, and to be honest they were surprised that I had gotten as bad as I had. It's a bit like I mentioned earlier. I didn't notice some of them had babies, they didn't notice I was appallingly addicted.

Some felt terrible they hadn't realised how bad it had gotten nor understood what was going on. But there was probably nothing they could have done about it anyway. Then there were the ones who were too scared to look at themselves, the ones who'd say, 'Ah, you weren't that bad anyway. You can have one drink, surely?' They stuck around for a bit, but they trailed off after a while. I was upset about this to start with as I felt abandoned, but they have their own journey ahead of them, and some of them don't suffer with what I've got, so they might be OK.

If you value the friendships you have and you don't want to cut them off, explain how important this is to you and that you need space and time to focus on building yourself up. If they truly give a shit, they'll understand and encourage you to do whatever it takes to put your recovery first.

A significant aspect of your recovery journey is building a network of sober friends. For many individuals struggling with addiction and alcoholism, feelings of isolation, loneliness and fear can be overwhelming. To continue using or drinking, many addicts and alcoholics distance themselves from caring friends and family, creating a cycle of isolation that's detrimental to their well-being. To heal from substance dependence, it can be highly beneficial to make connections and develop a supportive network of individuals who understand your journey.

Sober friendships are important, as they can help to overcome the loneliness you may experience when you set out. It's important to surround yourself with people who share the same goals and understand how difficult this is. They can help with the commitment you've made. They can keep you accountable, without nagging or coming across as sanctimonious. They can listen to the stuff that's going on for you and help you solve issues without resorting to doing something risky, assuming they've had the same experience as you. They can help with the big life-decision stuff. It's daunting making new friends, and you'll be taking a risk, but a support network is so important, especially in the early days. These friends can be the people that get you through another day.

Continuing the relationships with your mates who are still actively using or drinking can be a much greater risk, one that might potentially lead to relapse. Knowing when it's time to reconsider these relationships can be painful yet pivotal for your healing process. It's advisable that until you're in a secure place in your recovery that you avoid some situations you might find yourself in. If you do need to see these mates because of birthdays, anniversaries and

CHRISTMAS EVE, NEW YEAR'S EVE

so on, you can always bring a friend along who's also sober so you're not on your own with it.

MY FAMILY AND FRIENDSHIP LIST

1. _____
2. _____
3. _____
4. _____
5. _____

WORK

Some of you might have been able to hold down a job in active addiction. I wasn't one such person.

Depending on what type of job you do, you might wonder if it's a good idea to let your employer know. Obviously if they put you in rehab they'll know all about you. Some jobs have health insurance that covers this, but it's not always the case.

If you've been drinking, taking drugs at work, using your work computer to access online porn or gambling, and you've been found out, it will be up to your employer to decide on the outcome, depending on your work policy.

Some industries in the past wouldn't go out of their way to discourage alcohol use; this was the case in the sector I worked in, where no one took issue with how smashed you got. However, this was a long time ago and I believe things have changed massively. At major music industry conferences there are now mental health initiatives, a mental health first aid course, and alcohol and addiction awareness talks; there are also members of the industry who found recovery, and they are up on podiums talking about it and the effects it has had in the workplace.

I'm really pleased that people are getting the support now, as this shift in attitude means they don't have to lose everything, as many of us did, and can seek the help they need without fear of judgement.

If you haven't yet been found out and have started to embark on your journey, it might be an idea to let your boss or bosses know. They can support you by cutting you some slack when things get stressful, and they might be able to make provisions when it comes to work events by providing non-alcoholic drinks, which have improved massively over the years due to the rise in people choosing sobriety as a lifestyle choice. But, of course, you don't have to tell them anything if that suits you. What you disclose is entirely up to you.

CHRISTMAS EVE, NEW YEAR'S EVE

If you've been unemployed for a while, you might be thinking of getting a job. Please remember that you're worthy of employment and that without you even realising it you will have tons of transferrable skills. It takes a lot of skill being a drug addict or alcoholic. Navigating addiction requires resilience, resourcefulness and adaptability – these are qualities that are invaluable in any job and, as much as you don't know it, you've mastered them. You managed to stay alive to this point, and that's a bloody miracle! My mate left his job to became an air steward; he flies all over the world now, going to an AA meeting in every city in the world he flies to. He's having a ball!

Starting a new job in recovery can be daunting. People are inherently curious and will want to know what you did before, why you don't drink and much else. You don't have to tell them anything if that suits you. What you disclose is entirely up to you.

Try not to rush into anything too stressful and take your time. As much as you'll need to be financially independent, your wellness comes first.

> **MY WORK LIST**
>
> 1. _____
> 2. _____
> 3. _____
> 4. _____
> 5. _____

CHILDREN

It would be remiss to write a book about addiction and the effects it has had on me and not acknowledge that addiction affects everyone, including children. So funnily enough, it's not all about me. I didn't have kids while I was in active addiction, but I'm a parent now and it's tough going some days. Most of the people I know, however, including my wife, did have kids in active addiction, although hers came away relatively unscathed. This is not always the case.

Living with parents who are struggling with addiction can negatively affect a kid's development in so many ways: socially, psychologically and emotionally. This can't be avoided. Addiction can create so much instability in a kid's life that it can affect their education, their relationships, and their own physical and mental health. We might not even realise this because we're so wrapped up in ourselves that the kids become invisible. They can't do the normal stuff that kids do – such as have their mates over for sleepovers because the house might feel so tense and unpredictable that they feel ashamed – and they may not have the same stuff as their friends because of the lack of money in the house, it having all been spent on drink and drugs. The pressure on kids is massive and they're faced with dealing with complex problems that are much too grown up for them to even begin to understand. They must deal with stigma, shame, guilt, all feelings that have been imposed on them, and they don't have the slightest say in any of it.

If you're a parent and you're in recovery, you might have lost a child to services and been out of contact with them for years. One of the best things I've witnessed in my time in recovery is the rebuilding of those broken relationships; dads reunited with their daughters, mums who've had all their children fostered or adopted getting the opportunity to rekindle the relationships they'd lost. I've known parents in recovery having to deal with their children suffering later down the line with their own addiction and mental health issues. And even though they struggle to come to terms with it, just because they've found recovery doesn't mean that one of their own can't set out on the same destructive journey that they did. The difference is that they are in a much better position than their own parents were to find and access help for their kids, and to right-size it.

Whatever the future holds for these children, there need to be honest, open communication and support systems in place to support them. And just like family and relationships, the process of gaining trust back will take a while, but you must just keep showing up, being present and committed, and change will come.

MY CHILDREN LIST

1. _____
2. _____
3. _____
4. _____
5. _____

CHRISTMAS EVE, NEW YEAR'S EVE

HOLIDAYS

I love holidays without the pressure of getting smashed. I'd dread going away, wondering how I was going to fill my days. Holidays used to consist of travelling to wherever I was going, making sure I had a few drinks at the airport, wondering how I was going to attempt to get whatever I had left from the night before through customs, then bottling it and sniffing everything I had before I got on the plane, which meant I was having a panic attack and sweating for the entire flight. I'd land, dump my bags, and then it was off out to the nearest pub, and that would be it. Not a sight seen, not a word of the local language learned. Buying nasty cocaine from dodgy local dealers who'd cut it with whatever white powder they could get their hands on, I'm sure my nostrils were spotless and hairless by the time I came home.

So my holidays were always a shambles. If I went with a girlfriend, I'd inevitably ruin them by getting wasted and failing to do everything I'd promised to do, and we'd end up rowing the entire time.

Fast forward to today, and my holidays have undergone a radical overhaul. Now they consist of seeing every sight available, walking for miles in the blistering sun, rowing boats with my daughter around lakes and traipsing around trying to find places to eat. My wife meticulously plans the itineraries.

She has everything planned: where we're going, how long we're staying and what we need to see. She books in advance, so we must turn up to these places on time, and we do every naff tourist thing possible. I recently went with her on a work trip to Berlin, and neither of us had been before. She had some shows she was working on in the evenings, but her days were free. Once we got there, we dumped our bags and went off exploring. She loves a shit statue.

We had friends that had travelled over to see the gigs, and we did go to a dodgy German bar afterwards, but at no point did it ever cross my mind to even consider not being back in our hotel by midnight so we could get up and go to the Nikolai Quarter and the Brandenburg Gate the following morning.

The key to this was planning and preparing. And that's what helped me. I made plans, I stuck to schedules. We didn't have the kids with us on that trip, so there wasn't a need to be rigid, but it was an opportunity to make the most of a city that we'd never been to.

When my wife got sober, she'd only go to countries that had tighter restrictions around alcohol. It just made it easier, knowing she couldn't get her hands on drink without it being a major hassle, so incrementally it became easier to go away. This sometimes still influences our choice of destination and type of holiday. They've shifted from being focused around people partying and getting wasted, to just relaxing and enjoying the experience. With holidays now, I make plans, I relax and I enjoy myself, as opposed to a week of sunburn, sweating, hangovers and sleeping in, missing out on life and experiences. My mates still go off on boys' holidays and my wife nags at me to go. I suspect she just wants a break from me, but I always turn it down. Instead I look forward to hearing the stories of absolute mayhem and disaster caused by a group of tragic middle-aged men who really ought to know better, and I count my blessings I stayed put!

MY HOLIDAY LIST

1. _____
2. _____
3. _____
4. _____
5. _____

AVAILABLE FOR BIRTHDAYS, WEDDINGS, CHRISTMAS, FUNERALS AND BAR MITZVAHS

Occasions, Christ, they're a minefield. I have written several articles over the years for publications that have reached out to me to ask for suggestions on how to get through Christmas and various other milestone occasions sober – or at least safely. And it's probably one of the most common questions I get asked on my social media. For a myriad reasons, big events can be extremely triggering. You might have ruined Christmas for several years in a row or turned up drunk to a family member's funeral and added to the upset.

I've listened to stories of utter madness from families who've had to tolerate drunk uncles behaving inappropriately, nans wetting themselves on the armchair and someone who actually pissed on the Christmas turkey, although gauging by what I hear about turkey, they may have felt it needed a bit more moisture.

But in all seriousness, Christmas can be isolating and lonely, and if you're hanging on by your fingernails it can be even harder. The idea of getting through these sorts of events can feel overwhelming and fill you with apprehension. And being around family at this time can be triggering.

CHRISTMAS EVE, NEW YEAR'S EVE

If you're not at the point where you've completely stopped, but you really want to, set yourself a target – a small, manageable, achievable, realistic target. These are referred to as SMART targets and can be applied to any given situation. If you start small, you might end up coming to the realisation that you feel much better and that you don't need to drink in order to be part of a gathering. It could be something like: I'm not going to have a drink on New Year's Eve, and give yourself a limit and try to stick to it. You could book a cab to make sure you have a time limit, and you'll be conscious that you've planned that exit strategy. Have one planned anyway, as you could end up feeling overwhelmed. You could also do things like bring your own non-alcoholic drinks, focus on your gratitude, and every time you turn a drink down give yourself the affirmation that you're doing good. Celebrate the small wins. Connect with others who are also staying sober over the holidays – you can all arrange to do your own thing.

Work nights out don't always have to be a big piss-up. Suggest an activity other than the pub, and anyone who wants to go can go afterwards.

You could give Dry January a go. Tell people you're doing it, which will make you accountable, and you'll probably end up being really supported and joined by others. The chances are you'll like the feeling of waking up hangover free, and that feeling could replace the desire to drink! Staying sober past Dry January might be a challenge, and for many Dry January feels like a trial run before they fully commit. An Alcohol Change UK survey back in 2021 reported that almost four million people took part in Dry January, but only 10 per cent of these quit for good afterwards. If you do find yourself reflecting on how much you drink during Dry January, for example, it might be a good time to start looking at the effects that alcohol's having on your health, finances and overall well-being. It's a time when you think about why you drink, what are your triggers and whether you even like it. All these questions you ask yourself will have an impact on you, and they'll hopefully lead to a place of better health and mood. And obviously your finances will start looking better!

MY OCCASIONS LIST

1. _____
2. _____
3. _____
4. _____
5. _____

Twelve

The Secret Drug Addict

Social media ... where addicts, alcoholics and emotionally unstable people are motivational speakers.

When most people kick off a social media account, they start with the best intentions. They might think they're going to change the world one post at a time. But as the followers pile up, something shifts. Ego can rear its head.

I never wanted to be social media famous. That wasn't my aim when I started the Secret Drug Addict account, nor was it when the follower count ticked up. It was never about money or attention for me. I wanted to share my story, raw and unfiltered, I wanted to vent my frustration at the government cuts to alcohol and mental health services. And I just wanted to post what I wanted without retribution. I wanted people to feel less alone with their struggles.

Over the years I've had lots of rehabs all over the world reach out to me to endorse and suggest their facilities, and therapists who have DM'd me asking me to recommend them to people who get in touch. I knew none of them, and they all offered me financial renumeration. But that's not what it was ever about.

The *Sunday Times* did an exposé on dodgy rehab brokers a few years back. They discovered that these brokers were taking upwards of 30 per cent of the fees, paying Google thousands of pounds to come out in the top three of their search results, and one company was registering with multiple different names. They would upsell add-ons like therapy, even if it wasn't required, and psychiatrists and GPs were shown to be taking kickbacks for referrals. It was vile, with nothing whatsoever trustworthy in it for desperate families. I decided to stay well clear of the unscrupulous sharks and snake-oil merchants, and do what I do because I was given support and help freely.

Don't get me wrong. I've got to keep a roof over my family's heads and I have kids to feed, but something about making money from another family's misery just doesn't sit well with me. Some families can afford the upwards of £28,000 that some of the more salubrious facilities charge; others beg, borrow and sell their kidneys to get their loved ones into a grotty rehab in an industrial estate on the outskirts of Luton. At first I was flattered that they thought I was influential enough to be worth approaching, but they don't care. It's just about their marketing and their bottom line. There are no guarantees that the family's loved one is going to stay sober when they get out of the magic twenty-eight-day programme, and no refund or compensation is ever offered. Whatever the outcome, that £28k is gone forever.

A lot of rehabs bought into this because the competition was so great, with some of the most well-respected and established rehabs being involved. The whole racket drives up the cost of care – that 30 per cent has to be clawed back somehow. It's like the Wild West, but instead of panning for gold, everyone's fighting over sick people trying to get well. Body brokering, as if it's a trading floor in the City.

The recovery industry is a goldmine. I worked in the music industry and dabbled in some low-level petty crime. But the addiction and recovery world are some of the dodgiest of the lot.

After the scandal broke in 2018, there was a lot of noise and pearl-clutching by the regulatory bodies, who called for the banning and regulating of the rehab brokers. Some states in the US had already done this successfully. Google did make a show, temporarily banning ads for rehab clinics. But once the media fuss died down, the circus packed up and moved elsewhere, finding further loopholes to exploit. The brokers now must be 'certified by Google', because Google, as we all know, are the real experts in addiction treatment.

The whole debacle was depressing. These are vulnerable people, people at their lowest ebb needing help. And what do they get? A system more interested in their wallet than their well-being.

This isn't just about money, it's about lives. When someone is struggling, timing is everything. That moment when they ask for help by verbalising is fragile and can be fleeting, but when they reach out for help their pockets are being dipped. The success of their rehab can be the difference between recovery and relapse, between life and death. It's not about pushing a bit of paper around and fighting over commission rates; these decisions have life-altering consequences.

We need real change, not just lip service and temporary bans. We deserve transparency, regulation and accountability, a system that puts people first, not the coffers of the bloody brokers. Nobody should have to risk this when their life is on the line.

Taking money from a rehab for referrals is dangerous territory for me; if a rehab offers me £1,000 per referral, staying ethical becomes impossible. This shit is not about the money; recovery saved my life, so why then would I put a price tag on something that was given freely? I'm just paying it forward. It must come down to what's best for the individual. They may not even need rehab; they might do therapy, go to meetings, detox in a clinic or at home. They might even do dayhab, which is rehab that's 9 to 5, Monday to Friday, as it might suit them better. They could be at home at night for their children, or whatever commitments they have.

If I recommend a therapist to someone and the therapist isn't that great or the right fit for them, but the therapist pays me and that person has a bad experience, then that's on me. With addiction, the risks are massive. A bad experience might mean someone never tries therapy again, and the consequences could end up being catastrophic.

THE SECRET DRUG ADDICT

This isn't like social media influencers pushing clothes or make-up. If a shirt they influence you to buy falls apart, you'll most likely bin it and move on. But in recovery, if someone has a bad experience, they might give up on getting help altogether. So it's not just about a substandard product, it's about a missed opportunity to get better.

If I had five rehabs that I knew of, and two of them were paying me a fee, I'd probably end up pushing the two that were paying me. It's just human nature. You'd like to think you were above it, but money can have a way of clouding your judgement. So the easiest way to avoid that is to just not get involved. It's about maintaining my integrity, even when no one's looking.

Instead, I might spend an hour on the phone with someone or give them bits of my time over weeks or months, in the hope that the time makes a difference in their life. Twenty minutes a week for six months could mean someone might end up making positive changes in their life and becoming a better parent, a better partner, a better employee. The potential benefits are literally endless, and for what? My time while I'm walking to school to pick my daughter up or at home having a coffee. It's a small sacrifice, and there's always a hope that it might make a difference in someone's life.

Sometimes this approach just doesn't work. I talk to a lot of addicts whose lives are properly fucked, but they're terrified of change. I totally get that. It took me over a decade of trying before I came to the realisation that I could change it all. There's a comfort in familiarity, even when it's devouring you whole. Drugs become your whole world, your social circle, your coping mechanisms, your everything. The thought of giving that up is terrifying.

When I first got sober, I filled the gaping hole left by drugs with Narcotics Anonymous meetings, soaking up the wisdom from the old timers who passed on their experience to the newcomers. It was a way to fill my time, keep the wolf from the door.

Using drugs takes up a lot of time and energy, and when your life has been consumed with waking up, using drugs and finding ways to get more drugs, then taking those drugs and so on and so forth, like a merry-go-round of misery, the time disappears quickly. This is particularly true when you don't know what hour of the day it is and you live an almost subterranean life, like a troll under a bridge. When you stop using, it leaves you with so much free time – time to reflect on all the crap, time to feel sorry for yourself, time to climb the walls bored out of your tiny mind. That's if you choose to do nothing; then of course it's going to be boring. So you'll need to find positive ways to fill your time.

One of the hardest things I've had to accept is that life for the most part is actually really mundane. When you've been conditioned to being surrounded by drama and living in crisis mode, the calmness can be uncomfortable. It's

THE SECRET DRUG ADDICT

waking up, going to work. Eat, sleep, work, repeat. The constant drama and adrenaline is not real life; the merry-go-round chucks you off. I don't necessarily help people to feel good, although I have to say it does make me smile when I get messages months, sometimes years later saying thank you and that after talking to me or just reading my social media posts, my correspondent has now taken responsibility for themselves and addressed their addiction issues. Doing my bit to help feels good, but it's not what motivates me.

Personally I'd be happy never speaking to anyone again and just hanging out with Dolly listening to Kneecap and watching old *Hannah Montana* episodes.

But there's something about passing on what I've learned that feels necessary when most of the services and resources that helped me live again have been stripped away, leaving only the likes of the body brokers and the other charlatans with their 'magic wands'.

In recovery I've learned to push myself out of my comfort zones, the ones that would have me alone, depressed and doing drugs. Most of the things I think I enjoy aren't healthy for me. Some days are harder than others; I feel like I'm fighting tiny fires in my head, and trying to find that balance can be challenging. It's often awkward and uncomfortable, but it's OK to feel that discomfort and it's not as crushing since I learned to ask for help. Most of my fuck-ups have come from fighting reality and not asking for help. The shit is always going to happen, it's painful and will only linger longer if I resist it. When I accept it and ask for help, my problems don't magically disappear but they often become less significant and less overwhelming.

I have to be careful not to get emotionally invested in the work I do as the Secret Drug Addict. It's hard, but if I did I'd spend a lot of my time being disappointed, because if I take responsibility for the people who get well, then, surely, I also have to take responsibility for those ones that don't. I'm just one person with a social media account.

My DMs are always open on every platform that I'm on. I sometimes miss things, as I don't have a content manager, although I have a wife who scowls if I post something too out there. She only knows when I do this because her mates will call and tell her; strangely enough, hers is one of the only accounts I've blocked.

On an occasion where I'd missed something, I was walking down the street and just checked my account on Twitter/X. A girl had gone off on a tirade of abuse, calling me a fraud; she appeared really angry and was publicly baiting me. I remember initially feeling really angry too, and felt like responding to her tweet in the same tone she'd tweeted me. I decided, however, to privately message her and apologise for ignoring her mum's DM, and I asked for her name so I could search my messages. I searched my inbox and found the message; I hadn't actually missed it at all – I'd tried to call her mum, but she hadn't answered. I always call from a withheld number to keep myself safe and boundaried. It's all I can do. She'd missed the call due to that fact, like loads of us do. The dispute was quickly resolved, she apologised and deleted her tweet calling me a fraud.

She gave me her number and I ended up speaking to her for over an hour. Earlier that month she'd attempted to kill herself and was obviously at a very bad stage of her life. Her using was out of control, her family had run out of ideas, she'd had no help from services and couldn't afford private rehab. I spoke to her about attending meetings; she'd tried recovery before, so I tried to convince her to go back. We kept in contact, and after a few months it seemed that she was doing quite well and was planning to come to a recovery convention in London. I go every year with my family because I like to listen to the speakers – it's also a good way for me and my wife to catch up with old friends who we might not have seen since the previous year's convention. This girl had come up with a group of people in recovery from the town she lived in, so she met me and also my family.

In early recovery it's often recommended that you stay away from romantic relationships with other people also in early recovery as it can be detrimental and distracting. Not everyone takes this suggestion on board, and Jenny – that was her name – was one of those. She got into a relationship with a guy who was out of prison and living in a bail hostel while attending meetings. He was instantly controlling and unable to stay sober, it got very messy very quickly and as a result she relapsed. It was bad enough that she was thrown out of her family home and ended up living in a hostel. She had gotten to ten months clean and sober, and here she was back at a point where she couldn't stop using and her life was in crisis again. She tried and tried, maybe reached two or three days, but ultimately she'd use and drink again.

    I had a call from her a few weeks ago, but it was maybe a pocket call. I stayed on the line just in case, not sure if she meant to contact me. I could hear a muffled conversation, the type you have when you're wasted, and found myself taking it quite personally. I felt myself resenting the time I'd given her and was angry at her because she'd relapsed, which was ridiculous. I'd forgotten that she wasn't well, and that I do this because I have a choice in what I do; my time is given without expectation of anything back in return. I forgot that eighteen years ago I was ignoring all the suggestions I received around relationships, and it was a bit rich. I felt for her mum, who had gotten to the point that she couldn't cope anymore. I still hope that one day she picks the phone up. I have hope, not expectation.

★ ★ ★

THE SECRET DRUG ADDICT

I set up the Secret Drug Addict account by accident. It was born from another account that I created when helping to set up a charity with someone who had all the best intentions but didn't have the first clue. It also didn't help that he was secretly drinking eight hours a day. The charity never materialised, and he ended up owing a lot of money to a lot of people, me included.

So I'm left with a Twitter/X account, and it has a few followers. I hadn't really dipped my toes into the platform as it always seemed a bit silly. At the time you could only work with 140 characters, which basically meant you could write a slogan and maybe a link to a news article. It was nowhere near as sophisticated as Facebook had become. But over time I started reading those linked articles: the austerity cuts to drug services, the PIP (personal independence payment) assessments, the bedroom tax, the two-child cap, all the services that disproportionately affected the poorest in society. It made me angry, so I changed the name of the account and got myself a cool profile picture.

I've always had socialist values. Not in a *Socialist Worker* way, but I hated injustice and prejudice, and the last Tory government were all about that. Yes, I understood that the economy was bang in trouble, but there was no mention of raising taxes on billionaires, and we had a lot of them at the time as it was before Russia's invasion of Ukraine in 2022. All of the cuts I was witnessing were affecting people like me, who make up most of the population.

I started tweeting articles as I read them, following accounts of the people that were making a difference and calling for change. And then I started using my voice. I attracted a bit of attention, which was strange. I started to engage with people struggling with the effects of the cuts, real-life people with real problems. I felt powerless to do anything, but I could give them suggestions, mainly ones I'd picked up from being in recovery. I was getting so much traffic on my profile that I was starting to think, what else can I do?

Neville Southall, the ex-Wales and Everton goalkeeper, got in touch with me. He had a Twitter account that had blown up due to his support of sex workers, LGBTQIA+ and mental health groups, and he told me about many of the relevant issues.

Mental health services were shutting at 5 p.m. and crisis teams were being cut to the bone, so he thought it would be a good idea to make use of his account and to always have someone there. So I took over the account between 10 p.m. and 2 a.m. twice a week, while also looking for other people to take over small independently run services, mental health charities, drug services – any campaign that had an agenda that fitted Neville's values and which needed a bigger platform to reach vulnerable people, and any resource for vulnerable people to find services and help.

THE SECRET DRUG ADDICT

This increased the number of people who started following me on my own account. I was finding so many people who'd fallen through the cracks, people marginalised by society who were unheard and voiceless, struggling with the effects of addiction.

So I opened my DMs, and that's when it started getting batshit crazy. Like Jenny's mum, I had hundreds of worried parents, unable to cope with their children's addiction and the effects it was having on their families. And when lockdown happened it all just exploded.

One of the first people who really affected me was a heartbroken mum. She was caring for her grown-up son, and at the time she contacted me she was scoring heroin for him. He'd been in a car accident with his fiancée, and as a result of his injuries, which were painful but not life-threatening, he'd been prescribed codeine. A lot of it. Before this he didn't have a drug problem: he was a normal young man from a town in the Midlands, had a normal job and was saving up for a deposit to put down on a house. Looking forward to his future. The accident caused him to have spasms that he couldn't control, and his pain was not going away. He was a young man, so they suggested that he attend pain management sessions and in time it might improve. The NHS appointments would be moved or cancelled, and there was no chance of surgery. He ended up losing his job – he had to sit all day at a computer and the spasms would be so bad that he couldn't concentrate.

He was now put on Disability Living Allowance (DLA), and the codeine continued. In the meantime his relationship broke down, a consequence of all the other consequences, and this spiralled him down into depression, so he was prescribed antidepressants. This went on for a few years.

He was called in for an assessment with Serco, who'd been contracted by the government to get people off DLA and back to work, or at least get them off benefits. The appointed nurse deemed him fit for work around the time he had a medication review with his GP, who removed the codeine prescription. His condition hadn't changed, yet his lifeline was taken away. No reduction, no tapering.

One of his mates gave him methadone – the details were sketchy around this, but he used it for a time. Then the supply stopped. This was a family who'd never encountered drug services or knew how to go about explaining the mess they were in. His mum knew that methadone was a heroin substitute, so went about trying to find ways to buy it. She'd go out in her car at night around the local estates and ask anyone who looked shady. This was a respectable middle-aged woman with no previous criminal involvement or connections resorting to the only thing she knew that could help make the pain stop for her son. She was trapped in this because there was no help available that she knew of.

THE SECRET DRUG ADDICT

I shared this story in a piece I wrote for a newspaper a few years back. They asked me to write a response piece to a statement that the health secretary at the time had come out with – yes, it's Sajid Javid; I told you I'd come back to him. He had a penchant for tone-deaf, downright offensive statements, which ultimately highlighted the distance between him and reality. He suggested, as we saw earlier, that it was families who could fix addiction issues. In a lot of cases, families are part of the problem, whether it be well-meaning enabling or causing the trauma that leads to addiction in the first place. Moreover, a lot of addicts don't have family around them for one reason or another, including that they may have been disowned years before. Rather than take responsibility for their failing government, the Tories passed the buck to overstretched, inexperienced family members to solve the problems. Which is why I ended up speaking to many of those families.

At the other end of the spectrum is Rod (by the way, all people's names have been changed to protect the innocent. I too am anonymous, after all!). Rod is someone I've known for several years; he's on a football forum I'm a member of.

I had an odd message from him a few weeks ago and he asked me to call him. I didn't call immediately because I thought it was going to be a lengthy discussion about a player who'd recently been injured, and I was in the middle of making dinner or something else mundane and normal.

I called him back a bit later, but he was at the gym so he asked me to call him in twenty minutes, but when I did he had another reason to not talk. This cat and mouse thing went on for a day or two, but we eventually caught up. I was in a bit of a bad mood over something and couldn't be arsed talking about football, but instead he starts talking about his wife, and how he met her for about fifteen minutes. Which was nice, but I was confused as to why he was telling me. He then started telling me about his cousin, who has recently been diagnosed with leukaemia. I let him talk.

After he'd talked for about forty-five minutes about everyone else, he blurted out that his wife was divorcing him. She was divorcing him, and one of the reasons she cited was his obsessive–compulsive behaviours. He was a hoarder, a compulsive hoarder of football shirts. Now this might seem a bit weird if you're suffering with drug and alcohol addiction. But addiction can involve anything that's harmful and causes pain and suffering. Rod was spending money they didn't have buying these shirts, he was secretive and he was dishonest about it. His therapist had told him he was an addict. But like a lot of people, he didn't understand this; he wasn't a heroin user and he wasn't pissing the bed after a bender. How could he be an addict when he barely drank and hadn't ever touched drugs?

His wife had been fed up with his behaviour for years and his failure to address the problem, and now she'd had enough. She was through with enabling his addiction and she'd put boundaries down, given him ultimatums, pleaded, bargained – all the things the loved ones of addicts who use drugs and alcohol do – and she went ignored. The consequences for him were divorce and losing the woman he clearly loved, because he simply could not stop shopping for shirts.

I remember as a kid we had a neighbour called Colin. He was a lovely guy who lived with his wife Pam and his daughter, a few years younger than me. One day they didn't live there anymore. Colin would go to work, wash the car at weekends and on the face of it was a completely normal guy, but he was a gambling addict. It turns out he started with scratch cards, won a grand on one of them and off he went. He was spending more and more money every week on these cards, but he never won more than a fiver. Then he tried his luck with horses, was terrible at that, so he turned to betting on the football.

I remember bumping into him a few times on the high street coming out of the bookies. That was where loads of the older guys used to hang out; it was like a social thing – pub, bookies, chip shop, in no particular order – so it didn't seem unusual. Not long after, there were burly-looking blokes knocking on his door, to no response, so they'd ask the neighbours if Colin was in. They'd just get shrugged-shoulder responses, but everyone knew full well that he was indoors.

Then the arguments started. You could hear them up and down the street. The neighbours would grimace and roll their eyes, but no one knew what was really going on. Then one day the removal men turned up on the street. Colin was nowhere to be seen, Pam back and forth to the van, face worn out from crying, their daughter playing with some of the other kids on the street.

Years later I found out that Colin's gambling problem had got so bad that he remortgaged the house to fund his addiction, had lost his job and hadn't been keeping up with the repayments, so the house was repossessed. That was my first experience of the damage of gambling addiction.

Since starting the SDA account, I've had hundreds of similar stories come through my DMs about people losing everything they own due to an addiction that hasn't been drug- or alcohol-related. It's easy to point fingers and blame all of society's issues on the vulnerable, it's easy to walk past a homeless person and create a narrative that they chose that lifestyle, they deserve it and were probably an awful person anyway.

Just because they don't look like you or act like they don't fit into the box, it's also easy to discriminate against the addicts with substance-abuse issues, missing the fact that it's a fine line. Addiction can affect anyone – your mum, dad, nan, aunty, teachers, politicians. It's non-discriminatory, it doesn't care how much money you have, where you're from, what you do, what race or religion you are.

THE SECRET DRUG ADDICT

That's why I'm anonymous. It's not because of the stigma of addiction. I always tell people that I've been sober a number of years. Especially in my real life. They think I'm cured and they think that's it. They trust me with the keys to their house, their workplace and so on. I've been socially accepted.

The reason why I'm anonymous is because I don't want to be social media famous. I don't want to be the poster boy for addiction. I mean, the reality is that I do want that – but I also want there to be no distraction from what's important about recovery and addiction. If I had a face, then it would be all about me. Equally when people say nasty things about me or the account it's not personal. It's directed at some anonymous account called the Secret Drug Addict.

After my brother died, I wanted to tweet about it – only a few people know me as me on Twitter/X. I put something out there so that people would know and they're aware in case they bump into me and ask me about my brother. I thought if I put it out there it would alleviate the awkward conversations and explanations later down the line. I had a mate ask about it in the responses, to which I'd replied that he should tell his mum and siblings and not worry about texting back. To which he replied OK, which is just what I wanted.

A few weeks later, the funeral was only two days away and I realised I hadn't even told my daughter. Suddenly I felt this need to tell her. She was going to be there, so she really ought to know. She'd never even been to a funeral.

So I wrote something for social media and left it in my drafts. I kept thinking to myself why I wanted to do this. I didn't want to reduce my brother's death to content. I felt uncomfortable with that, but I needed to understand the urge. Posting something about my brother's death from a drug overdose would get clicks and give me an endorphin buzz from the engagement. I knew this was going to be popular and it would be something to feel good about. I ended up tweeting something about it but then I muted it; I didn't want notifications to keep popping up reminding me about it.

Soon afterwards there was something about a Tory party gathering at Chequers and the drugs scandal there. I think they found traces of cocaine or something like that. I made a comment, and someone out there tweeted me back something about my brother and the drugs problem. He said my brother was probably the one who sold them the drugs.

First, I got angry and thought about how I was going to respond. I could have annihilated him online. But then I thought, *What is going on in your life that made you want to say that? Why would you say something so nasty and personal so publicly?* In the end I felt sorry for him and ignored it.

I've had a fair share of abuse. I've been called a junkie and a cunt, but the account is a buffer. So when people say unkind stuff I'm able to deal with it by dissociation. The phone doesn't define who I am. Some other people on social media who've set themselves up as influencers and experts – they've positioned themselves as that, so they're forever trapped in that personality. If you're a mental health influencer, for instance, you can never get better.

And I understand this; it's what I felt posting about my brother. You become defined by whatever it is that you do. And I suppose I'm not, because it's not really my name or personality there. I think with these influencers and experts, their boundaries lower over time because their brain kind of goes, you know what, this will get loads of engagement and I'm going to film myself rolling around the floor crying.

Sometimes I get people who message me about their unmanageability, their overwhelm, and I start by asking them about the practical stuff. Have you brushed your teeth today, did you make your bed, have you drunk enough water? Sometimes it can be the simplest action that changes a person's outlook on their life. When you're in a crisis, it's hard to see a way out. I find a lot of my work is reminding people about the practical stuff that they can do. I know I certainly must remind myself about all this stuff regularly. I'm just one person with a social media account, but I'm also a work in progress.

Maybe just doing those positive things without any expectations of receiving anything back is the only way to do this job. It's the only way to keep going and be of use to someone. It benefits me but it also allows me to be helpful to other people. It's important to my recovery – doing something good regardless of what the outcome is, without any expectation or reward.

Thirteen

Manifesto

The goal is that one day the majority of people will think of addiction as a health issue.

My life, in all its tedious splendour, feels full and busy now, not with the manic highs and lows I had when I was using, but with a steady and genuine fulfilment.

For the most part I've found pleasure in routine and the predictability of normality. I realised that the excitement I went out of my way to find was really just a distraction from my constant discomfort and self-loathing, and that real happiness was in the most mundane things.

Recovery for me certainly isn't a linear path. There are major setbacks and painful struggles, and there are quite a few days when you want to tell the world to fuck off. I'm not perfect by any stretch of the imagination; it's tough trying to always do and say the right thing, and I often don't get it bang on.

But each day I stay sober is a win. Life isn't always just about surviving and launching miserably from one day to the next. I'm learning to embrace the boredom because it would seem that's where life really happens – in those small, seemingly insignificant moments that all add up.

When my mum died ten years ago, it was incredibly painful. But getting through grief without drugs was a real human experience that I never believed was achievable. I felt every moment of it, every sharp edge, every dull ache. It wasn't pleasant, but it was real. It's like the difference between watching a film and being in it – you feel it in your stomach, your bones.

I've realised that even in mundanity, when you're not experiencing something profound, you start to notice small things. My daughter's laughter, after she's just said or done something silly. She's one of the funniest people I know. The conversations about future career choices, and how ridiculous they can be. There's a lot of eyerolling, but I'm bloody grateful to be present enough to listen to the nonsense.

I have two coffees in the morning to get me started, that's my routine. I can't have any more because I'm self-aware enough to know they spin me out. And if I forget, I'm reminded about it. I have a normal job, working with people who are nothing like me, but I have more in common with them than I ever thought I would.

I'd be lying if I said I didn't miss the excitement, the mad nights out, that feeling of invincibility that came with being wasted, the anxiety that came with scoring, the anticipation of that first sniff, the way the world seemed to slow down and speed up all at once.

But I know now those moments were brief, fleeting moments in what was an incredibly sad and empty exist-

MANIFESTO

ence. The cost was too high. The damage didn't just affect me, but the lives of people who gave a shit about me. That's not the legacy I want to leave.

Sometimes, I catch myself reminiscing about the past, about times when everything seemed easier because I was too numb to actually face my problems. But now I have a family of my own, and I know what matters. I want to be there for them, fully present, warts and all.

Helping others in their recovery is part of that choice. It keeps me grounded, it reminds me of where I've been and where I don't want to return. It's not about being a hero or a saviour. I haven't got a God complex – I'll leave that one to the other loons. It's about passing on the support I received, about being part of something bigger than myself.

When I help someone else, I'm helping myself too. It's like reinforcing the foundations of my own recovery. There's healing in connection, in knowing you're not alone in your shit.

It's so easy to feel isolated when you're in the depths of addiction, to think no one understands what you're going through, that you're the only person having that experience. But when you reach out, when you share your story and listen to others, you realise that you're not having a unique experience and that we're all in this together. That's where real change happens. In the spaces between people, in the moments of shared understanding and mutual support.

And yes, sometimes I still want the easy escape, the quick fix. The reminders of addiction never really go away. They're always there, whispering in the back of my mind, one pair of trainers at a time. But I remind myself those thoughts belonged to a kid who didn't know better, who was running from his pain instead of facing it. These days I'm learning to face it, to sit with it and to find healthier ways of coping.

Life isn't perfect, and neither am I. I still make mistakes, still have days when I wonder if it's all worth it. But I'm learning to accept the imperfections, to find clarity in the struggle and to hold on to hope even when things get tough. That's what recovery is about – not just staying sober but creating a life worth staying sober for. It's about creating something meaningful out of the wreckage of my addiction.

In the past eighteen years I've found strength I never knew I had. I've found power in being vulnerable, in owning my weaknesses and asking for help. I've found strength in being honest, in facing the truth about myself and my actions. And I've found peace in acceptance, in acknowledging that I can't change the past, but I can shape my future.

And while it's not always easy – in fact, sometimes it's fucking hard – it's always, always worth it. Every sober day is a win. Every moment of genuine connection, every laugh with my daughter, every small kindness I can offer

MANIFESTO

to someone else in recovery – these are the things that make life worth living.

What you need most in recovery are patience, honesty and acceptance. There are obviously a few more attributes you'll need along the way, but they all go hand in hand. If you're struggling to accept you have a problem with alcohol, drugs, porn, shopping, gambling and all the other areas and behaviours that can cause damage to your life, you're not going to look to fix it, are you? Honesty is a big one, and I don't just mean lying to others, although that's a big part of it. I mean being honest and true to yourself. It's admitting that you're struggling, that you're tempted and triggered, because if you can't even be honest about that, how are you going to deal with it? There's absolutely no shame in this. If anyone told me that they put down their drug of choice and that was that, never thought about it ever again, I'd call them a liar to their face, then ask them what they replaced it with.

You are going to think about it. It was a huge part of your life. You'll have regrets about the shit you missed, the money you wasted, the time you wasted. I missed my entire twenties, lost great jobs, lost friends; I'm fucking angry about it. But can I get them back? No. Do I move on and make the most of what I've got now? Sometimes, not always but mainly yes.

The same goes for feelings. You're going to have to accept how you're feeling. Be patient with yourself.

Feelings are like the tide – they come in and then go out again, and you can't control that.

Things change.

If I can just accept that this is how I feel today, it's not going to last, and maybe tomorrow it'll be better, and this feeling will shift. Maybe it won't change tomorrow, and it'll be shit for a week or two. I know there have been times in the past where I've been as happy as a pig sitting in its own excrement and times where I've felt like just giving up. When I was the piggy, it didn't last forever, and when I felt like giving up, that feeling also didn't stick around. I learn to take the bad with the good and appreciate the good a bit more when it's here.

And that's something I never had when I was using. Everything felt so permanent. If I felt bad it felt like it was always going to feel that way. When I lost my job, I was utterly defeated and totally devastated. So my using ramped right up to the point where it was all-consuming, and rather than try to salvage something out my career, I allowed myself to be dragged under. But no one took me to one side and told me that this didn't have to be the end, that my life wasn't over because I'd lost a job. Maybe if I'd had someone to tell me that, I wouldn't be here trying to piece a book together, so maybe it's the universe's way of telling me it had other plans for me.

Now I know that feelings pass, they're not always facts. And although sometimes they take longer to pass

MANIFESTO

and they can be uncomfortable as fuck, they will eventually depart.

It seems recently that people seem to expect recovery to be almost instantaneous. This is a bit like waking up one morning and thinking, *Fuck, I've become a fat bastard*. You didn't just wake up overweight, did you? Didn't go to bed slim and wake up four stone heavier? Nope, it's been insidiously creeping on, bit by bit, inch by inch, and you've not really noticed it. Then one day you're trying on an old pair of jeans and suddenly the fuckers don't fit anymore, and you're left wondering how that happened. It's a tough reality check.

It's the same when it comes to addiction. You don't wake up one morning a full-blown addict. It sneaks its way in slowly. An extra drink here and there, a line and a pre-drinks drink before you leave the house to go out for the night. Before you know it, you're in it, neck-deep reliant, craving and chasing a bit more to get you back to when it worked the first time around and it felt fun.

But just like weight, there's that moment when it hits you.

Maybe it's your bank balance, you're late for work again – that's even if you bothered to go in – or you've missed another family gathering. Again, like the weight gain, you wonder how the fuck you got to that point. So you drag yourself to the gym, empty the cupboards of junk food and go a bit mad for a week. Although you don't see the four stone fall off in that week, if you leave it there, you're not going to see any change, are you?

It's about keeping at it, day after day. It's all the little steps, the mind-numbingly boring, repetitive actions that add up.

Like I said, you won't notice anything for a while, but then one day you look at yourself and think, *Oh, I don't look as crap as I did*.

And that's very much what recovery is like. You don't just go to one meeting or take a day off drinking and suddenly you're cured, it's a miracle and all that shit. No, it's laborious. You've got to keep showing up, keep doing the work, even when it feels like nothing is changing. Because believe me, it is. You might not see it day to day. But all those little steps you're taking amount to something.

Recovery is the same deal: you have to keep chipping away at it, and slowly things become easier to handle, more manageable. You build up a resilience, like muscles you didn't even know you had. Even when life gets tricky, you have a better handle on how to manage it. In my early recovery I'd get really upset about the smallest things. If someone looked the wrong way at me, I'd be ready to go to war. But as time went on I got better at managing my emotions. I got better at life.

Looking honestly at my life, there has not been one single thing that has been improved or enhanced by me getting drunk or stoned. Absolutely nothing.

MANIFESTO

If I have money worries, drinking my last quid is certainly not going to sort them out. If my wife is nagging me about my unmanageability and thoughtlessness, a line of coke isn't going to make her stop. Quite the contrary. It's insane thinking.

I unsuccessfully tested that theory for years.

There were so many times when I thought, I'll just have one line, it'll take the edge off, or one spiff to relax me. It never did. All it did was prolong the inevitable and make everything a hundred times worse when I finally had to face my problems. Because that's the thing about getting sober. At some point you're going to come face to face with the shit you've avoided your whole life.

I can't emphasise enough about those small steps, the little wins. You keep turning up for life and then one day you realise you're living it. You're getting through the day without needing a crutch, you can deal with your issues head on, you can enjoy the good stuff and have memories of it.

I can't remember the first real crisis in my recovery, there were so many to start with. I lost my house, I ended up in a hostel, I was a car crash around women, my dad was a pain in the arse.

All these things were fucking terrifying if I'm honest. Some of them I dealt with badly, resorting to old behaviours. This time I couldn't avoid them. I was wide open and vulnerable. Everything in me would scream *Run away*, but thankfully I didn't.

I asked for help and got through all of it. I felt incredibly proud of myself after I did that, because it was never something I thought I could ever do.

My recovery is not just about not using, it's learning to live on life's terms. It's about growing up, facing your fears, getting your house in order, turning up and being present for someone other than yourself. It's bloody hard work, considering that the word 'altruism' wasn't really in my vocabulary eighteen years ago. The work you put in will be absolutely worth it and the freedom that comes with this immeasurable. It's the type of freedom that's about knowing you can handle whatever the fuck life throws at you.

I said at the top of this book that everything that I know about addiction and recovery could be written in a 280-character social media post. When I was approached by a publishing house to write a book about addiction and recovery, I'd never even considered writing a book and it wasn't something that particularly appealed to me. It was so far out of my comfort zone and my cripplingly low self-esteem, and my addict head tells me that I'm not good enough. Then I thought it was someone winding me up. Why the hell would someone want me to write a book!

I know a few writers, so I asked them and it all seemed legit. But then there was the actual process of writing the thing.

MANIFESTO

I left school without a GCSE, so how the fuck was I even going to write a book? What do I talk about? It comes so naturally to some people, the flow, the content. It's easy when you know how.

But my reality is I don't know how.

My wife encouraged me, came to meetings and read the contract, while I was just frozen in fear. What if it's shit, what if I can't do it? What if my daughter reads it when she's older and disowns me? What if someone criticises me publicly, tells me it's shit and calls me a fraud?

This entire process has been one of the most uncomfortable experiences I've ever had. Writing paragraph after paragraph, trying to recall people I've encountered over the years, deciding on which ones I wanted to talk about, worrying if they'll identify themselves and be angry. But the reality is that most people who approach me all have a common thread running through their lives and their tales as old as time.

Talking about my vulnerabilities, my losses and my family life has also been uncomfortable, making me look at my past – and the shame around it – and face my fears head-on.

Eighteen years ago I came into recovery broken into tiny little pieces because I didn't know how to do life without drugs, from the start of my working career to the very last day I used. Drugs had been a pivotal part of my life, and they'd ruined me.

I was angry, resentful and bitter at the people who had fucked me over and abandoned me, at the industry that had spat me out without a safety net when I was a kid, and at everyone who had a duty of care towards me when I was a kid and missed the signs. But the bedrock of it all was fear. Fear that I wasn't good enough, I wasn't worthy of love, of nice things or happiness.

I bought a whole set-up in lockdown to start a podcast. It was something I thought would be a good idea, but I couldn't think of the right format I wanted, so it was packed away and so far has never seen the light of day. My wife gets really annoyed at me about it because of the expense of another one of my impulse buys. She's also frustrated because she thinks I'm more than capable of doing it, but a mixture of complacency and apprehension has got the better of me.

And that's the thing: writing a book about addiction and recovery without any training is terrifying. I've always been careful to not give instructions and just try to offer advice and suggestions. I try not to focus on absolutes, because years of therapy have taught me that you can lead a horse to water, but you can't make it drink. Everyone whom I've helped over the years has come to the solution for themselves.

I'm not an evangelist, nor an advocate for any model of recovery. I just know what worked for me.

And then there's the words. How many words do I

MANIFESTO

know? I can talk, like, a lot. I'd hope that I'm articulate, but writing this book has made me question that. I've actually had to resort to a thesaurus to find alternative words from time to time.

At every point throughout this process I've doubted myself. I've questioned myself, I've laboured some points, I have driven my poor wife mad, I've had my deadline for submission of the manuscript extended.

And the reality is that I'll never think it's enough. I'll wake up in the middle of the night and think about something I should have said, someone I should have talked about, an experience that I had that was profound yet hasn't been included. Or I've missed a charity out in the help section because my brain was switched off at 2 a.m. after spending hours focusing on something less important.

I started my account to help people in their darkest moments, as hanging around social media sites at two in the morning made me realise that there are a lot of people in real crisis, people who have no one to turn to. It had such a profound effect on me that I decided to give my account as much attention as these unheard people deserved. I didn't set it up to monetise it or get famous. This is bigger than me, these are people's lives and they need to be listened to, not be used as a stepping stone to further an online career.

If I ruled the world I'd have this stuff talked about in schools more, as it needs to be discussed openly rather than be shrouded in a cloak of stigma and shame. These conversations need to be normalised. They need to be family dinner conversations. Addiction can affect anyone. It doesn't discriminate, and most people know an addict or an alcoholic.

I'd provide decent health care to addicts and alcoholics that didn't cost the earth, as well as free therapy for them and their families until they were at the point where they were fully functional human beings who contributed to society in any way they chose.

So going back to 'What if it's shit?' and 'What if I can't do it?', we can add: 'What if my daughter reads it when she's older and disowns me?', as well as 'What if someone criticises me publicly, tells me it's shit and calls me a fraud?'

Well, I've been told worse. I've sat in meetings for eighteen years and spilled my guts, opened old wounds, even cried at points. What I've learned is that it's not about the result; it's just about trying your best and the outcomes will be what they will be. Focus more on the actual journey rather than the destination.

And the fact is that the Secret Drug Addict is not the only thing that I am. I'm a dad, a husband, a son, a brother, a friend and an employee, and I've worked really hard to be the best I can be at all of these roles.

Social media might be full of addicts, alcoholics and emotionally unstable people posing as motivational speak-

MANIFESTO

ers. But real recovery, real growth? That takes place in my day-to-day endeavour to stay sober, to be present and to help others. It's not glamorous, it's not going to make me rich and it's not always tweet-worthy, but it's authentic. And at the end of the day, that's all that matters.

My Twelve Steps

STEP 1: GROUNDS FOR DIVORCE

Denial in addiction is like telling yourself that the biscuit won't ruin your diet or I'll just watch one more episode and go to bed, but the biscuit is another glass of wine and the TV show is another line, and the diet and your bedtime are your life. Recovery doesn't kick off until you admit the obvious, because let's get it right, you're not the one in charge here. Drugs and alcohol are running the show, and that's like leaving a bunch of escaped monkeys in charge.

STEP 2: FAITH

Now is the time to get comfortable believing in something bigger than yourself. Call it God, Santa's elves, the Universe or 'that mysterious force that keeps Netflix running at 3 a.m.'. It really is whatever works for you. The point is: if you're relying on willpower and your own track record, well … you can see how that went.

STEP 3: HELP!

This isn't about waving a little white flag and giving up – it's more like handing over control of the steering wheel before you crash into a parked car at 2 a.m. It's handing yourself over to something or someone who has your back. Let a higher purpose take the wheel and veer the car away from that poor, unsuspecting parked car. You wouldn't go to a psychiatrist for a broken leg, would you? This is the same principle.

STEP 4: I'M STILL STANDING

This is like taking a microscope to yourself and looking inside your soul. You get to ask yourself questions like why did you do what you did, when you only 'intended' to have one drink, but your 'actions' were 'Whoops, three-day bender' and something went wonky. This is where you get to work on fixing that shit and start coming back to life.

STEP 5: GIVE ME SOME TRUTH

It's time to fess up. Usually, you'll do this with someone who's been where you are, so never feel like you're the

MY TWELVE STEPS

worst person in the world. You're not! Yes, it's going to feel awkward. Yes, you'll feel vulnerable. But getting honest is like unblocking a toilet – disgusting to start with but, oh, the relief afterwards.

STEP 6: DON'T THINK TWICE, IT'S ALL RIGHT ...

This may not be obvious to you right now, but nobody's perfect. You've got good bits, excellent in fact, but you probably have some bad bits and some downright questionable bits too. Stop beating yourself up and accept the whole package. And besides, perfection is boring and so much maintenance! Keep a bit of you in there.

STEP 7: I WALK THE LINE

Unfortunately, and downright shocking, it would seem life isn't all about you. Asking for help doesn't make you weak; it makes you smart enough not to try juggling the rabid cats alone.

STEP 8: LANDSLIDE

Make a list of people you've wronged. Chances are it will be long. And no, you can't skip your ex. Don't get into the guilt-wallowing here – this is a chance to fix things, genuinely. I'd like to say that it always goes to plan. It doesn't. You have no control over people and how they react or respond. What other people think is none of your business; you do you.

STEP 9: ALL APOLOGIES

Let go of old grudges. Cling onto resentment is like drinking poison and hoping they die. Release it, get rid of that shit, breathe it out, talk it out – not too much, though – and move on.

STEP 10: MAKE IT EASY ON YOURSELF

Keep check on yourself. Think of this step like maintenance, like you would have done on a car. Doing this regularly will prevent breakdowns. If you feel these on their way, refer to the **HALT** questions: Am I Hungry, Angry, Lonely or Tired? There's a good chance it might

MY TWELVE STEPS

just be one of those that are the catalyst to tip you over the edge.

STEP 11: CONNECTION

This is when you and the thing you've chosen as your higher power sync up. You might work out what your purpose is, or at the very least finally start believing in yourself and that you're worth more than just binge eating and binge-watching TV. Your life takes on meaning. Again, this is not going to happen overnight. It may not be a bolt of lightning. You might wake up one day and find meaning in things you've never noticed before.

STEP 12: TEACH YOUR CHILDREN

This is about giving back. Sharing what you've learned, helping others and building a life that you're proud of. It's like paying rent for living on Earth with kindness, not cash.

Acknowledgements

Thanks to Pete Wilkinson, Helen, Ian Longwell, Ray Badejo, Kiki Machado, Chris Rowe, Tommy Morris, Andrew Worzel Worsley, Mike the Bastard, Chris Tofu, Sue and Nick Mercer, Dougie Papworth, Eve Gonzalez, Melissa Gordon, Patrick Walden, Roger Sargent, Tara Robinson, Barry Dickins, Steve Zapp, Bill the Mod, Barbara Saitch, Saad, Sandie, Westy, Pani, Bob Dylan, Titanic Café, Conal, Paul, Alan Pell, Neetsy, my daughter, my wife, my stepsons, Ruth Nelson, Alun German, Andy Allen, Andy Bell, Dan Ferguson, Chris and Darren Germain, Lisa Cullen, Charlie Creed-Miles, Charlie Dawson, Neville Southall, Erol Alkan, Martin and Susanne Horne Liam Óg Ó hAnnaidh, Naoise Ó Cairealláin, J. J. Ó Dochartaigh, Daniel Lambert, Roy and Geri Jenkins, Roger Hunt, Keith Mullen, Juliana De Angelis, Matthew Sutton, Sally, Russell and Penny Roberts, David Fehily, Kaan Gulcelik, Christian Nochall, Paul Hutton, Steve (Kid) Jansen, Saffron Lashley, Tony Adams, Gareth Moloney, Jah Wobble, Phil Payne, Dick Green, Muff Winwood, Dawn John, Emma Taylor, Johnny Hopkins, Manuel J. Waldner,

DIARY OF A SECRET DRUG ADDICT

Dominic O'Ryan, Russell Sedman, Ian 'Longwell' Aitchison, Maisie Nelson, Ciaran Boyle, Ruairi Boyle, Eren Gulcelik, Paul Husband, Miles Jacobson, Steven Young, Eko, Mark Larter, Frances Giblin, Ginger Al, Christian D'Acuna, John Peel, Kathleen Hanna, Maya Hanika, Graham Stuart, James Brown, Kevin Rowland, Jermaine Robinson, Gary/Graham, Caroline O'Connor, Ann Gibson, Hakan Gulcelik, Pembe, Paul Gallagher, Peter Allum, Chris Price, Paul McKay, Chris Lahr, Isaac Vallie-Flagg, Alan McGee, David Baddiel, Jeremy Thomas, Utah Saints, Tom Ward, Sean Sutton, Clive Anderson, Ajmul Khan and Ester Fester.